OUTGROWING CHURCH

Outgrowing
CHURCH

If the Law Led Us to Christ, to What Is Christ Leading Us?

Second Edition

John Killinger

 CASCADE *Books* · Eugene, Oregon

OUTGROWING CHURCH
If the Law Led Us to Christ, to What Is Christ Leading Us?
Second Edition

Cascade Books
An Imprint of Wipf and Stock Publishers
199 W. 8th Ave., Suite 3
Eugene, OR 97401

www.wipfandstock.com

PAPERBACK ISBN: 978-1-5326-9277-2
HARDCOVER ISBN: 978-1-5326-9278-9
EPUB ISBN: 978-1-5326-9279-6

Cataloging-in-Publication data:

Names: Killinger, John, author.
Title: Outgrowing church : if the law led us to Christ, to what is Christ leading us? 2nd ed. / John Killinger.
Descripton: Eugene, OR: Cascade Books, 2019. | Includes bibliographical references.
Identifiers: ISBN: 978-1-5326-9277-2 (paperback). | ISBN: 978-1-5326-9278-9 (hardcover). | ISBN: 978-1-5326-9279-6 (ebook).
Subjects: LCSH: Christianity—Discipleship. | Christianity—21st century. | Christianity—Forecasting.
Classification: BR121.3 K48 2019 (print). | BR121.3 (epub).

Manufactured in the U.S.A.   10/03/2019

*This book
is affectionately dedicated
to all the "new," "next," "progressive," "emergent"
Christians trying to find their way
in a cultural world
where the old church,
the one with which most of us grew up,
simply isn't up to the job*

Contents

Introduction

In one sense, we never outgrow church. It is too big, too impacted with meanings both ancient and modern, too rich in its heritage of art, literature, and philosophy, for anybody to outgrow it. It would be silly to speak of outgrowing it if we meant that we could outgrow these things in any serious way.

But we do outgrow our own sense of church, or the sense of church to which we made a commitment of sorts at some specific earlier points in our journeys, and we do outgrow certain manifestations of it that haven't kept pace with our own developing quest for holiness and adventure. Surely any persons who are more mature and knowledgeable today than they were yesterday have outgrown the church in which they grew up, especially if that church only barely met their needs at earlier stages of development.

And, when this happens, it is incumbent on the serious pilgrim to move on, to experiment, to discover some new and different experience of church, if possible, that will satisfy his or her needs at the next stage of existence, and thus justify having begun with church at all.

My own life has been inextricably involved with the church.

I became a professing Christian when I was eleven and felt a call to the ministry when I was sixteen. I attended a Christian university, and, after earning a PhD in literature at a secular graduate school (I was pastoring a church at the time), went to Harvard Divinity School for a master's degree and then to Princeton Theological Seminary for a second doctorate.

In all, I have pastored eight churches, two of which were rural charges and another two of which were in the major metropolitan areas of Los Angeles and New York. I have also taught in four major American theological seminaries—Vanderbilt, Princeton, Chicago, and Claremont—as well as in three Christian colleges or universities.

I have actively belonged to four of the major Protestant denominations—Southern Baptist, Presbyterian (USA), Disciples of Christ, and the National Association of Congregational Christian Churches—and my final stint as a minister was in the Reformed Church of America, as Executive Minister and Theologian at the famed Marble Collegiate Church in New York City.

I also spent a year as Theologian-in-Residence at the American Church in Paris, France, an ecumenical church related to the Office of Overseas Churches of the National Council of Churches in the United States.

So the reader can appreciate that I am steeped in church and everything it implies. From the age of eleven, I have never known anything else. My entire life has been lived on the altar of Christian service. When I married, it was to a young woman who was active in the church as an organist and pianist, and we were in church together for more than half a century. Almost all of our friendships were in church. When we reminisced, it was usually about church. But before my wife died in 2014, we felt that we had pretty much outgrown the church—or at least the church as it existed in most places in America. We grieved for it, and circled it still like animals circling a spot where their forebears lived and perished. But we could not resurrect it, or even its ghost, in palpable terms that satisfied our hearts.

Too much was missing!

My first thought about writing this book arose from the haunting title of Barbara Brown Taylor's *Leaving Church*. Taylor, an Episcopalian, finally got a little pastorate of her own, in the hill country of North Georgia. Apparently it was a blissful experience that ran aground when she began to tire of the minister's all-consuming schedule. So she left, but with no ill thoughts about the little congregation she had pastored. Her situation, in fact, sounded idyllic.

But I read her book at a time when I was between churches and beginning to wonder if I could stomach another. I had had some idyllic experiences too, especially in the first small churches I pastored. Comprised mostly of farmers, small business folks, and a few teachers, those churches were warm, friendly, and cozy. But I had also pastored a number of larger churches where things weren't always so happy. For one thing, they usually had traditions that were onerous and punishing, especially for ministers who found them sub-Christian or at odds with humanitarian instincts. And, for another, they always contained some members who were direct descendants of Genghis Khan, Rudolf Eichmann, and Lizzie Borden.

It is an odd fact, borne out in the lives of many retired ministers I know, that most pastors can hack the tough duty at these sub-Christian churches a lot better when they're in there fighting against the lack of Christian faith and love than they can later when they have to find a place to worship where they are no longer the leaders. That's when it hits the fan for most of us and we balk at even attending church, much less belonging to it.

I have a dear friend who recently retired from the United Methodist ministry in a Southern state. He couldn't wait to hang up his spurs and become an ordinary church member without portfolio—until it happened. Then he began the arduous job of finding a church where he could feel comfortable in worship on Sunday. It wasn't long before he was in despair.

"I can't stand it," he wrote in one e-mail. "The music is lousy, the minister's sermon is worse, and there doesn't seem to be an ounce of Christian love in the whole congregation!"

A few weeks into his retirement, he took a two-day-a-week job at a pizza restaurant, preparing salads and delivering pizzas to the oven. Within a short time, he had become the *de facto* chaplain of that restaurant. People were coming to him for counseling, they had stopped cursing so much in his presence, and he was happier than I had ever known him to be in the pastorate.

In my own disenchanted time since leaving the ministry, I began thinking that Taylor didn't go far enough with her book. Somebody, I thought, needed to write about *outgrowing* church, not just leaving it. That was my problem, I realized. I hadn't just left church, I had actually outgrown it.

I didn't know this until I quit beating my head against the wall, trying to turn churches that were basically secular social clubs into real, matter-of-fact churches where a godly spirit prevailed and people dealt with one another in love and compassion instead of envy and rancor. But it was true. Suddenly I realized it was time for me to actually walk on from the church as an organization and stop hovering around it hoping to find something that would rekindle my excitement from the old days.

And then I realized why a lot of people haven't been going to church. Not just people who once belonged, but people who never went at all. They have outgrown it. The times we live in, the education we get from the media, our electronic connectedness, the sense of being world citizens and caring about the earth and its diverse inhabitants, all conspire to put some people out in front of the church, which can be reactionary, narcissistic, and generally unloving and unreceptive to people who aren't like the ones that belong to it.

Books on Church Leaving

What surprised me, as I began thinking this way, was that there were already some books appearing whose message was similar to the one blinking in my brain. They weren't all from authors with the same background I had, as a pastor and theologian, but they were saying essentially what I was thinking, that sometimes the only thing you can do on your spiritual pilgrimage is to leave the organizational entity that gave you your start in the first place.

As long ago as 1993, William D. Hendricks published *Exit Interviews: Revealing Stories of Why People Are Leaving the Church*. Even then, claimed Hendricks, an average of 53,000 people a week were leaving the church, most of them complaining about its lack of real spirituality. Some were going to other religions such as Buddhism and Islam and a few were joining parachurch spirituality groups, but most were simply evaporating from the rolls, concluding that churches would never measure up to their own professed standards.

In 2002, New Zealander Alan Jamieson published *A Churchless Faith: Faith Journeys Beyond the Churches*, examining the same phenomenon of countless Christians vanishing out of the official churches in order to become servants of God in other places.

Researcher George Barna's *Revolution* studied the data on church-leaving for approximately twenty years and concluded that roughly one-quarter to one-third of all Christians in the United States are now allied not with a local church but with some parachurch organization such as a house church, a prayer group, a witness band, or a social services organization. They had grown tired of talking about church, he said, and wanted instead to *be* the church. Barna predicts that by the year 2025 U.S. churches will have on their rolls only about half the Christian population of America, and the other half will be actively involved in groups and activities not officially sponsored by churches.

Brian Sanders's *Life After Church: God's Call to Disillusioned Christians* describes the church as "a failed experiment." People who have fallen in love with God, he says, aren't happy with what they're getting in their local churches, so they often feel the call of the Spirit to seek other places of worship and service. His own final Sunday in church, he says, was the one when he sat in the pew bored by a pastor talking about how the church's bathrooms needed to be redecorated. "I knew at that moment that would be my last Sunday."[1]

A lot of people continue to go to church long after they've found out how boring it is. But Sanders didn't want to be one of them, shopping around and "consuming" churches the way Americans consume everything else. He left church the way a lot of people do these days, in order to follow God in a commitment most church members only talk about.

Sanders understands the predicament we are in when we are finally ready to leave the church. On one hand, we cannot have church alone; there isn't any such thing as the church of one, there is only the church in community, the church as the body of Christ. But, on the other hand, if the church isn't fulfilling its mission as a radiant fellowship in love with both God and the world, it cannot satisfy the needs of the person who really wants such a church. So what can an honest seeker do except leave?

Julia Duin's book *Quitting Church: Why the Faithful Are Fleeing and What to Do About It* echoes many of the things these other authors had already said. As religion editor for *The Washington Times*, she has been in a good position to observe church joiners and leavers during the last decade. What she sees is a lot of people who are finally admitting "the banality of the local church" and who have given up on it despite the fact that they continue to read the Bible, pray, and lead devoted Christian lives. Young people especially, she says, aren't willing to stay with an organization that is "just reinventing the wheel" and not doing anything to change society. They have left the little church on the corner for "the First Church of Starbucks."

---

1. Sanders, *Life after Church*, 19.

Duin believes the sexuality issue is responsible for many people's unhappiness with church these days. Because of evangelicalism's negative attitude toward gays and lesbians, many younger members in its churches feel caught in a hypocritical situation; they have gay and lesbian friends at work and in their social life but are compelled to remain silent on the matter in church.

The same is true, says Duin, about most conservative churches' views on women. If women can be CEOs of major corporations, why can't they pastor churches? She cites a 2006 issue of *Christianity Today* that ran a cover story on how Reformed theology is sweeping conservative churches. In an accompanying photograph, all the pastors were men. Nor did a sidebar listing all the leaders of the Reformed movement contain any women's names. "How many female authors," asked Duin, "have appeared on the cover of *Christianity Today*?"[2]

The Emergent Church

In addition to these books, there has been a spate of activity from authors either involved in or impressed by the so-called "emerging church" phenomenon: Brian McLaren's *A New Kind of Christian* and *A New Kind of Christianity*, Robin Meyers's *Saving Jesus from the Church*, Diana Butler Bass's *Christianity for the Rest of Us* and *A People's History of Christianity*, Michael Spencer's *Mere Churchianity*, and Phyllis Tickle's *The Great Emergence* ranking among the best of them. Tickle's book deepens and dignifies the movement by locating it in one of the great epochal transition eras for the church, thus identifying it with the century following the fall of the Roman Empire, the century at the beginning of the high Middle Ages, and the century of the Reformation, during each of which the church in general underwent enormous changes as it adapted to new cultural factors.

2. Duin, *Quitting Church*, 144.

The common theme running through these extremely well-written and interesting books is the need for the church today to be flexible in the face of enormous socio-cultural shifts, so that it doesn't choke inside its own moral and theological carapace while there are exciting new worlds to be approached with the gospel of the kingdom of God. They represent the need for Christians in this vibrant era to travel lightly, taking only what they absolutely need from the wreckage of the past and being willing to follow the Spirit into new places and alliances.

There is as yet no available information on how many people have actually left the church because of its moribund institutionalism and unwillingness to adapt to the times, but as a percentage of those still clinging to the wreckage of the mainline churches it is probably very small. I live only a few miles outside Washington, DC, and travel extensively in the U.S. and abroad, and, aside from a few more liberal and essentially small congregations that do not express any highly visible rejection of big-steeple religion, I have not encountered a single church where there is any real discussion of emergence or progressivism as a primary intention of the community.

When I discovered how much had already been written about the exodus from the churches, though, I confess I wondered if I should even attempt to write a book called *Outgrowing Church*. Obviously a lot of people have already had the same idea. And the emerging-church authors have cogently and articulately covered most of the reasons for being critical of the church as it has been and seeking another, more creative way for Christianity in the future.

Room for One More?

Still, I am prompted to write my own story and express my own dissatisfaction with the church I have known, for several reasons.

First, I am probably the oldest writer among those I have mentioned, and have seen and experienced more varieties of Christianity than they. Ordained to the ministry at the age of eighteen, I have pastored in my lifetime eight churches, from small, rural congregations in the hills of Kentucky to sophisticated big-name, conspicuous-wealth, and old-power churches in Los Angeles and New York. Three of the eight churches were Southern Baptist, one was American Baptist, one was Presbyterian (USA), two were Congregationalist, and one was Reformed Church of America.

Between pastoring tenures, I have been a professor in seven seminaries and universities, where I have taught students from almost every conceivable denomination and religious background—from Baptist, Presbyterian, Episcopalian, United Methodist, Disciples of Christ, and Roman Catholic to Holiness, Assemblies of God, Independent Christian, and Seventh Day Adventist. Being a professor of preaching, I have had far more engagement with students at the personal level, through their essays and sermons, than professors in other areas, and have heard the stories of their individual journeys with both sympathy and fascination. In fact, years later, I still maintain contact with dozens of them via the Internet, monitoring their lives and their thinking on a fairly regular basis.

In the 1970s, when the winds of change were stirring in both Protestant and Roman Catholic ecclesiastical circles, I was teaching courses at Vanderbilt Divinity School in experimental preaching and worship, urging my students to think freshly and creatively about their responsibilities as liturgical leaders. In 1974, I published a book called *The Second Coming of the Church*, in which I discussed the church's great burden of its own institutionalism, the possibility of a new birth for Christianity based on the use of sensitivity training (which was then the rage in secular therapy), and the promise of the electronic age as a stimulus for thinking outside our diminutive theological boxes.

In that book, I told about a recent encounter with a close friend who was minister of one of the most prominent churches in America, and how suspicious I became from his manner of speaking that his personal integrity and allegiance had been suborned by the huge responsibilities he bore as leader of such a large congregation. Probing, I asked how living with those responsibilities, especially politically and financially, now skewed the sermons he preached and the stands he took as a pastor on such sensitive issues as war, race, and poverty. At first he hedged. But at last he looked me in the eye and confessed, "It's a hell of a dilemma. If you say what you think ought to be said, you know it will alienate a lot of people who make the style of this church possible. If you don't, you sort of lose touch with yourself. You just have to work out the compromises as you go. And besides, these rich SOBs need somebody to minister to them too."[3]

Eventually I asked the question, "Is the church hopelessly moribund? Can the church not somehow regain its perspective and integrity so that its word counts for more in the human community? Is the church so ridden with the very evils and inadequacies it seeks to rout out that it can get no leverage at all on the human condition, and must therefore be content to be another weak voice crying in the wilderness of the world's pain and confusion? Is the church so much in need of the gospel that the gospel is put to shame every time the church tries to speak of it? Can the church which has talked so egregiously of salvation these many centuries now hope to be saved?"[4]

The jury is still out on this. I tried to manifest my own faith in the church by leaving seminary teaching in 1980 to become pastor of a large Presbyterian congregation across town from Reverend Jerry Falwell, where I soon learned what it costs to speak out for real openness, inclusiveness, and freedom.

3. Killinger, *The Second Coming of the Church*, 11.
4. Ibid., 13.

So in a way I have been struggling with the problem of church renewal as long as anybody I know. I appreciate the work of the younger pastors and theologians now speaking out about new forms of discipleship both inside and outside the church. Like them, I do believe the church will survive for centuries more, but, unlike many, I don't think it will be a quick fix. On the contrary, I think the church—the *real* church—will probably exist as an underground movement, maybe in homes and storefronts and office suites, for a long time before it emerges as anything resembling the network of public congregations we have known in the past. Institutionalism is an important thing, in one sense, for it enables us to grow and spread and relate the way any organism does; but it also inevitably becomes *pro forma* and self-serving after a certain period of time, usurping the very life of the spirit that brought it about in the first place.

A Step Further

There is one more thing that will possibly justify the publication of this book among so many decrying the failures of the contemporary church and its outworn approach to moral and theological issues. That is that it goes further than the other books in its willingness to suggest that Christianity may well need to *supercede itself* in order to serve its real purpose in the future. Almost every author to whom I have alluded thus far inevitably returns to Jesus as the church's only marker. This is surely justifiable, given that the church is the institutional extension of his life, teachings, and ministry. But what if it is time to understand Jesus as a signpost and not as a destination?

Michael Spencer's *Mere Churchianity*, which is an eloquent indictment of the church for going off the tracks from original Christianity, speaks about our proneness to idolatry, and how wrong ideas about God can themselves become false gods.[5] Then he goes on to say: "The false gods need to be replaced by the one true God who comes to us in the teachings, example, and power of Jesus of Nazareth. The short course in Christianity can be spelled out in a few words: Jesus is God. Lord and God. God revealing himself to human beings. The God-man. God in a bod. God in human flesh. God as a baby, a carpenter, a Jewish healer, a crucified falsely accused criminal, a risen conqueror, and a reigning King!"[6]

Brian McLaren, almost always a very precise and careful theologian, admits in *A New Kind of Christianity* that "We are stuck with Jesus, and he won't go away."[7] And one of his imaginary dialogue partners in *A New Kind of Christian* swore fealty to Jesus as the unavoidable Lord by saying, "I really believe that not one person will be in real contact with God the Father apart from the work and wisdom and love of Jesus. If I didn't believe that, I don't think I could call myself a Christian."[8]

Even Robin Meyers, who calls "Jesus was God" "the dominant American heresy,"[9] builds his entire summons to a reconstruction of Christianity in our day around the singular person and ministry of the Nazarene, insisting that what we need today is "Jesus wisdom, not doctrine."[10]

I do not wish to quarrel with these fresh and original thinkers, for they exhibit signs of hope for a more flexible and earnest Christianity in the near future. But I do not think they go far enough in their willingness to part from the orthodox heritage of the churches they criticize. Once one admits that Christianity in its more popular forms today has misread the Bible, as they do,

5. Spencer, *Mere Churchianity*, 34.

6. Ibid., 35.

7. McLaren, *A New Kind of Christianity*, 240.

8. McLaren, *A New Kind of Christian*, 65.

9. Meyers, *Saving Jesus from the Church*, 93.

10. Ibid., 158.

then it is time to move beyond the arrant christocentrism that has marked the church since it erected its theology on the Fourth Gospel, with a pre-existent Christ, a God incarnate in human history, and confess that our former intransigence on this point, while it may have served the church well in some ways, has proven a nonnegotiable stumbling-block in our attempts to move beyond Christianity's imperious "our-way-or-the-highway" attitude to a more universal understanding of God—the God of all peoples—transcending our pernicious and outworn doctrines.

I will come to my arguments for a signpost-Jesus later. Meanwhile, it may be important to establish my credentials for those arguments by describing the journey I have made as a Christian, and this description, along with accompanying observations, will occupy the earlier chapters of the book. I am now a retired minister—a clergyman without portfolio—and, like thousands of my compatriots, I am free to visit various churches on Sunday morning and make my own assessment of what seems to be transpiring in them. Frankly, it has not been an edifying experience. I have joined the ranks of disgruntled parsons who all seem to complain about the emperor's new clothes as they pass from church to church.

I have to ask, why are thousands of retired ministers lost and unhappy when their work is done and they can't find suitable congregations with which to worship? I'm not kidding about the number. Most ministers no longer in harness find it almost impossible to experience a sense of the divine presence in the churches they attend. They drift from one to another like AA members in a room full of alcohol-free bars. They yearn to worship, but can't. They become spiritual zombies, wondering if everything they worked for—the whole success of Jesus's church—was only a joke or an illusion they were the last to get.

I'm not too worried about young Christians who leave the church because they've got high octane in their tanks and most churches are trying to get by on a cheap brand of regular. As far as I'm concerned, they're actually seeding the world with Christian idealism, and that's good. The church's loss is the world's gain, so to speak. And Jesus himself would have been out of most churches before you could say "Judas Iscariot."

The thing that bothers me has nothing to do with the numbers on church rolls or the drain evangelicalism is presently feeling from losing its bright young men and women to some parallel universe of spirituality. What upsets me is the way church is imploding today because it can't transcend its own institutionalism to invent a new faith for a new day. It is obviously so tied to its old images and traditions that it can't reconceive its mission in terms of a global technological culture where *every* old form is either dead or dying, regardless of how strong or central to everything it once was.

It also bothers me even to speak of outgrowing the church, because, as I said, my whole life has been wrapped up in church. If I sound elegiac at times, it is because I feel a profound sadness at the fact that I live in an age when most of us, by dint of everything we've read, heard, or absorbed from the media, have indeed outstripped the church in which we first learned to believe and worship God. We have learned to see God in a million places where the church doesn't acknowledge God, and to apply the church's ancient wisdom to modern problems with a passion seldom felt in all of history. We are ready to step into the future at a time when the church appears regretfully unable to sacrifice its past.

What I Would Like to See

I shall not, in this book, counsel anyone to leave the church. I don't need to. Those who feel the pull to higher things require no encouragement from me.

What I should really like, if I could be granted one gargantuan wish, is that readers of this book would instead attempt to make a difference in their churches so that in the end they and others will not feel compelled to leave them. Half a millennium ago, it was the Reformers' cry to "Let God be God!" I would love to see thousands of readers of this book and others like it take up the cry today of "Let the Church be the Church!" It would thrill me to see something like the Occupy Wall Street demonstrations carried out in all the churches in Christendom, with parishioners camping out on the steps of their churches, sitting in the aisles, crowding the altars, and generally demanding something new and spiritual and relevant from their pastors and educators.

This would of course require that we do a kind of Vatican II in all our churches, of whatever denomination, and reform ourselves to meet the challenges of the day. It would mean some hard reconsiderations of the nature of God, in which we listen to voices from every land and culture, and, refusing the constraints of our tired old theological nostrums and catch-phrases, become vitally gripped by new, progressive, and imaginative understandings of God and God's relationship to the world.

At the same time, it would mean inventing a whole new language with which to talk about this God, a language far less anthropomorphic than the one we've always used, and one capable of expression to the populations of the fresh new world coming into being all the time. And out of all of this would grow a brand new way of worshiping God, of confronting transcendence and having our lives renewed and reoffered to God and to others in the very act of thus confronting it.

It won't happen overnight, of course. What's the slogan, "The difficult we do immediately, the impossible will take a little longer"?

But as an inveterate churchgoer hungry to remain involved in the church's life from day to day and age to age, I think I could ıgaged by any church that produced even slight evidence that s attempting to fulfill this mighty order. I need only see occasional glimpses of the church's being the church, of its striving to be what it can't easily accomplish, and I shall be satisfied.

I would love to go to church, come home, and write to friends and say, "I had a wonderful experience at church today. I heard a brave sermon in which the pastor attempted to come to grips with a scriptural text and ended by saying that she thought we have come further in our moral understanding today than the text had in its own time, and afterwards I overheard some deacons speaking with one another and agreeing that their pastor was right, and it meant they needed to discuss it further in their meeting to see what implications it might hold for the way their church attempted to become the church of Jesus Christ in our own day. We may never get to the finish line with this gallant idea, but it is exciting to me to be among Christians who are open to trying to get there, and I can tolerate our slowness as long as we are making the attempt. We are, after all, only the church in the way, and I find it highly unlikely that we shall ever consummate here on earth the dreams we have of a great and shining ideal."

That's all I ask. Not a perfect church, but one that is striving to be more perfect. One that confesses its sins and reaches for the stars.

Not a New Quarrel

I realize as I write this that I have been engaged in a lover's quarrel for a long time, wanting a deeper, better, and more faithful church. An early book, *For God's Sake, Be Human*, was about making Christianity real in our daily lives and not just faking a religion the way our parents did. One chapter, "Reading the Bible as a Human Document," called for a more honest approach to the scriptures, and brought Billy Graham, then a defender of biblical literalism, to Waco, Texas, the home of Word Books, to demand that Jarrell McCracken, Word's president, remove my book from the marketplace or face a boycott from the relatively new Christian Booksellers Association. McCracken refused, and the boycott was put in place for two years.[11] In the 1970s, when a few congregations were clamoring for more contemporary services, I published *Leave It to the Spirit,* in which I described the new liturgies springing up in Christendom and the possibilities they offered for a truer, more dynamic worship of God. This was followed by *Experimental Preaching* and *The Eleven O'Clock News,* collections of sermons, mostly by my students, that often employed shock tactics to enable normally apathetic congregations to really hear the gospel in our time.

In preparation for my seminars on experimental preaching, I often asked students to provide sensitivity exercises for putting us in the mood to think creatively. One of these exercises remains vivid in my memory. Two students on assignment that day, a husband and wife team named David and Glenda Webb, decided to initiate us into body-painting. They brought a sheet to lay on the floor and an array of finger-paints for decorating volunteer class members. One of those decorated that day was a fifty-something, balding, highly dignified Welsh clergyman named Geraint "Gary" Jones. Gary, who had been captain of a British Merchant Marine vessel during World War II, was pastor of a local Presbyterian church. Like a good sport, he followed David and Glenda's instructions to remove his shirt, shoes, and socks, roll up his pant legs, and lie on the sheet with arms and legs spread-eagled. David and Glenda began the painting job, but soon had everyone involved in putting designs on Gary, who, having surrendered to the spirit of things, was relaxed and enjoying the sensation of being colorfully decorated by his classmates.

11. One of Word Books' volumes was excepted from this measure. Keith Miller's *The Taste of New Wine* was too big a bestseller for the CBA to take it out of their stores.

When I ran into Gary several years later, he had left his pastorate to become headmaster of the famous Webb School in Bell Buckle, Tennessee, and then an equally prestigious private institution, Westminster School, in Atlanta. He told me that the experience of being painted by his fellow students in that class changed his life. "It freed me to be me," he said. "It helped me get rid of a lot of my old inhibitions and begin to live with real enthusiasm. I've been a different person ever since."

Small group techniques were springing up everywhere, particularly in business circles, where they provided ways for people to get to know one another beyond the usual superficial exchanges. My wife and I helped to initiate a small group based in a Presbyterian church we attended, and I wrote about this experience in a book called *All You Lonely People, All You Lovely People*, which encouraged the forming of new groups in other churches. During the months we were in this group, I also wrote a book for the General Board of Education of the United Methodist Church called *To Meet—To Touch—To Know: The Art of Communicating*, which received possibly the largest readership of any book I ever wrote.

During that time, I was serving on a task force for the World Council of Churches to restudy the meaning of salvation in our age. Headed by Dr. David Randolph, the task force met several times in various locales to brainstorm and share our ideas about salvation. Under the stimulus of these meetings, I wrote a book called *The Salvation Tree*, in which I discussed the multi-dimensional nature of salvation as we understand it in the contemporary world, touching on its relations to education, psychology, economics, sensuality, politics, and other important factors.

The Importance of a New Spirituality

As I dealt with future pastors and visited many congregations across the U.S., I began to see the importance of a new spirituality as part of the mix for any truly successful Christian congregation, so I began offering a course for seminarians in prayer and spirituality. Out of this interest grew the book *Bread for the Wilderness, Wine for the Journey* and four volumes offering a devotional approach to the reading of the Gospels.[12] My prayer seminar also led to another book on prayer and spirituality called *Prayer: The Act of Being With God.*[13]

I have mentioned *The Second Coming of the Church*, which was a very hopeful book, delineating ways in which the church could renew both its message and its methods. But by the end of the millennium, when I published *Preaching to a Church in Crisis*, I was reading the writing on the wall for a church that, in W. H. Auden's words, "would rather die than be changed." (In fact, I originally called the book *Preaching in the Last Days of the Mainline Church*, but, fearing repercussions, the publishers altered the title.)

One last reference in this boring litany of titles: In 2007, I published *The Changing Shape of Our Salvation*, in which I reported on my conversations with many ministers and congregational leaders across the U.S. who had already given up on the kind of personal salvation ballyhooed by evangelicals and fundamentalists to embrace an understanding of redemption that was more ecumenical, showing a willingness to embrace peoples of other

12. Killinger, *Bread for the Wilderness, Wine for the Journey: The Miracle of Prayer and Meditation. A Sense of His Presence: The Devotional Commentary on Matthew; His Power in You: The Devotional Commentary on Mark; The Gospel of Contagious Joy: A Devotional Guide to Luke;* and *The Gospel of Eternal Life: A Devotional Guide to John.* These four volumes were later published in a single book, *A Devotional Guide to the Gospels*, and this book was enlarged and republished as *Day by Day with Jesus: 365 Meditations on the Gospels.*

13. Killinger, *Prayer*; republished in 1993 as *Beginning Prayer.*

faiths, and more community-oriented, emphasizing the social nature of the Judeo-Christian faith and rejecting the idea of a God who seeks the punishment of ignorant or wicked human beings.

In other words, I have been in sympathy with the concerns of the new or emerging church proponents for a career now spanning more than fifty years, and hope this entitles me to express my present judgment on whether the church has become doctrinally obsolete and incapable of transforming itself from a centuries-old larva into a radiantly new and glowing butterfly. At the risk of telegraphing my punches and fueling the reader's desire to hurl this book away without reading another page, my answer is both yes and no. Perhaps I am like that seminary professor of whom Michael Spencer speaks so fondly in *Mere Churchianity*—I suspect it was Dr. Dale Moody—who used to burst into class with the announcement, "Tear up your notes, I've changed my mind!" My own ambivalence has to do with an indomitable hope that God can always start a new fire in the rubble of our human failures, and thus rescue us from the winter of our own discontent.

1

Outgrowing a
Particular Church

There's no way to keep going on this adventure . . .
without the community of Jesus around me, attempting
the same project. None of us can do this alone.

—MICHAEL SPENCER, *MERE CHURCHIANITY*[1]

All these years later, the way many of us are
doing church is broken and we know it,
even if we do not know what to do about it.

—BARBARA BROWN TAYLOR, *LEAVING CHURCH*[2]

Although I would hate to be condemned to attend it for the remainder of my days, I shall always have a fondness for the church I loved as a boy. It was a wonderful congregation to grow up in, and provided me with a lot of heroes, both biblical and contemporary. I admired the mostly gentle, sweet-natured people who belonged to it. They were good to me at a time when I needed them. They smiled at me, stroked me, and made me want to be a

---

1. Spencer, *Mere Churchianity*, 44.
2. Taylor, *Leaving Church*, 220.

worthy person. When I felt a call to ministry, they doted on me and made wildly magnanimous predictions about what a great preacher I would become. One elderly lady who had traveled to New York was sure I would become the minister of Riverside Church or the president of Union Theological Seminary.

That was heady stuff for a boy who still woke up with pimples on his face.

I left that church the way most young people leave their original churches, by going off to college and never actually returning to my hometown except to visit. For several years, I did go back occasionally, and always felt overwhelmingly welcomed when I did.

Then the church got a new minister who was even more of a conservative than the one under whom I'd grown up. He was in fact a militant fundamentalist. At the start of a worship service, he would sweep onto the podium like a superhero arriving just in the nick of time, drop to his knees by the pulpit in a semblance of deep, intense prayer, and then take charge of everybody—and I do mean everybody—for the next hour or hour and a half. The sheer force of his personality would not be brooked!

By this time, I had gone to Harvard Divinity School, where the famous existentialist theologian Paul Tillich was teaching. I'm sure the new pastor was aware of that, for all Baptists seemed to know who the world's greatest heretics were. Some were praying for them, and others were saying there was no point, as there was no prayer that could possibly save them from the fires of hell.

At Harvard I became a friend of Dr. Theodore Clark, a professor from New Orleans Baptist Theological Seminary who was spending his sabbatical year studying under Professor Tillich. Ted's wife Lois had a job and couldn't leave New Orleans, so he was alone in New England. My wife and I invited him to dinner frequently and we developed a warm, meaningful relationship.

Two or three years later, when I was teaching at Georgetown College in Kentucky and Ted was back home in New Orleans, Anne and I went down to spend Easter with him and Lois. It was while we were there that Ted was summoned to the office of the seminary president, Leo H. Eddleman, and told that the board of trustees had just voted to terminate him because of a heretical book he had published, *Saved by His Life*. *Saved by His Life* was no more heretical than a garden gnome, but Ted understood that his book wasn't an issue at all, only a subterfuge. The real reason he was let go was that he had spent a year at Harvard studying with Tillich. Baptists were afraid of Tillich. He was German (this was only fifteen years after World War II), was an exponent of existentialism, which few Americans understood, and didn't use the old evangelical catchwords to talk about salvation.

After going through this experience with Ted, I knew how my new pastor at home felt about me. He was always reasonably polite—he knew I had a big following among the home folks—but there was an edge of uneasiness behind his cheery voice and pasted-on smile. I could tell he was about as sincere as an American tourist in a French café professing that he really was fond of escargots.

Because I was naïve, I didn't realize then that the members of that congregation had invited that particular Baptist minister to be their pastor because he believed—or professed to believe—exactly what they did. I had not, until then, thought of doctrine as being a divisive force in a congregation. I assumed it was something for discussion, not something to fall out about. That congregation tolerated me because it had produced me. I was a son of its bosom. But the new minister was actually a very hard-nosed fundamentalist who was treading softly because of my peculiar chemistry with his congregation. He actually believed—and soon let people know he believed—that Christians should shun those who didn't agree with them, and treat them as heretics and outsiders.

Eventually, I realized that was what I was—a heretic and an outsider.

The funny thing was, it didn't shame me to be those things. It seemed like part of the natural order of my growth, a natural consequence of my religious pilgrimage. I went off to college, then graduate school, then divinity school. I had grown by all these experiences. I had brushed against some of the greatest minds in the world, in books and in real life. I had tested my beliefs against theirs. Sometimes I agreed with them and sometimes I didn't. But the encounters had definitely changed me. I was no longer the simple-minded adolescent I had been the day I packed the black cowhide suitcase my parents gave me for my seventeenth birthday and went off to college.

When I finally realized that fundamentalist pastor represented the thinking of most of the people in the congregation I loved, I felt sad. It didn't seem fair to be separated from people I cared about by the things I had come to believe and understand differently from them. Yet that was the way it was, and there was nothing I could do about it. I couldn't reverse what had happened and return to who I had been. That would have been unthinkable—and impossible even if I had thought it.

So I tucked the sadness down in my heart, the way a person puts a sandwich in a briefcase, and went on.

I still have a soft spot for those dear people who were so good to me. But I knew, after only a few years, that I could never return to that church and listen quietly to the sermons I once heard from the pulpit or agree in my heart with the prayers I heard offered by the old men of the congregation.

I was on a journey, and there was no turning back.

Many years later, I would write *Ten Things I Learned Wrong from a Conservative Church*. That was the church I had grown up in. I said in the introduction to the book how much I respected the members of the congregation where I grew up, and how much they meant to me personally. But then I outlined the things I had been taught there and had to unlearn along the route of my pilgrimage. Things like the literal, word-for-word inspiration of the Bible, the impossibility of going to heaven without Jesus, the primacy of males over females in the kingdom of God, and the equating of spirituality with not drinking, not dancing, and not being homosexual—all central to the life and thought of my old church but no longer tenable for me.

Someone told me recently that the minister of that church when *Ten Things* came out—another radical fundamentalist—had pronounced me a heretic and forbidden any member of the congregation to read my books. That particular pastor didn't remain long in his position, because he proved too harsh and overbearing for the congregation, and when he left they acquired a milder, more conciliatory minister.

In retirement, my wife and I considered moving back to our hometown to be near members of my wife's family who still lived there. But we had to think long and hard about such a move, and finally decided against it, for we were aware of some folks there who still shared the opinion of that earlier pastor.

A Sense of Freedom

For me, as I said in *Ten Things*, the most crucial issue in the profile of a church is where the minister and people stand on the inspiration of the scriptures. If they regard the Bible as a collection of ancient documents bearing witness in differing degrees of insight and faithfulness to the nature and glory of God, and not as a book of infallible nostrums and inerrant sayings, then I am perfectly comfortable among them. But if, as has proven increasingly true of churches in most denominations during the last few decades, they hold that God inspired the Bible verbally, word for word and book for book, so that it becomes a conspiratorial web of divine

5

revelation in each and every part, with some obscure text in the book of Leviticus bearing as much weight of inspiration as the four Gospels or Paul's letter to the Romans, then, no thank you, that offends my sensibilities—indeed, my sense of reason—to the point of a total turn-off, and I know I could not sit idly by without commenting on the outrageous offense that is to my very notion of God as a creator with intelligence, imagination, and, yes, even a sense of humor!

There was a time, in the beginning of my pilgrimage, when I could accept the full, verbal, plenary inspiration of scripture as a doctrine governing how I should read the Bible. But once I began to understand how the scriptures were written—Genesis by at least two or three authors, each successor redacting the work of his predecessor; Deuteronomy not by Moses, for it describes his death; the history books by hagiographers and demonizers; the Psalms by numerous authors, not solely by David; Isaiah by at least three different authors; Daniel by someone who lived later than he pretended to live, so that he could be sure of scoring some correct "predictions" about the future; the four Gospels by writers with very different perspectives and agendas; the Pauline corpus sometimes by Paul and sometimes not; and Revelation by an author with a fanciful imagination for concocting a symbolical and unreal future for true believers—I could no longer submit to such an idea. For me, it became not only immature and even ludicrous, but counterproductive to the life of holiness and true discipleship.[3]

At some point—I have often tried to decide whether it was during my days as a graduate student in literature or my years in divinity school or my tenure as a pastor who preached from the scriptures Sunday by Sunday—I realized that I had simply and finally outgrown the church of my childhood and its teaching

3. For readers who would like to explore the origins of the Bible, I can recommend Bart Ehrman's *Misquoting Jesus* and *Forged*.

regarding the most central issue of transmitting the faith. It was probably not dissimilar to the experience of a spouse who one day wakes up and realizes, "My God, I am married to someone for whom I have absolutely no affinity, and with whom I am never likely to agree on even the smallest, most inconsequential matter! What shall I do?"!

I have described my pilgrimage in *Winter Soulstice*—how I floundered for several years because I didn't have to make an irrevocable choice, going to a Presbyterian church, then a Disciples of Christ church, and, eventually, because I felt an urge to leave seminary teaching and become a minister again, accepting the call of a Presbyterian congregation that felt comfortable and manageable to me. I did have one brief flirtation with a large United Methodist church in Winter Haven, Florida, that wanted me to be their preaching minister. But Bishop Earl Hunt nixed the appointment because he said it would demoralize his other ministers if he permitted a plum like that to go to an outsider, and I realized anew why I hadn't become a United Methodist before, because I couldn't submit to the capricious will of an ecclesiastical boss.

Once loosed from my Baptist moorings, I was fated to feel always somewhat bereft of family, and have ever since felt envious of ministers who maintain their denominational allegiance. But the upside of it was that I was free to go wherever a church appeared to be most compatible with my personal beliefs and idiosyncrasies at that particular stage of my journey. Thus, when my time at First Presbyterian Church of Lynchburg, Virginia, drew to a close, I was happy to assume the leadership of the First Congregational Church of Los Angeles, and wasn't discombobulated by the change of polity such a move entailed. By then, I had become a radically free agent, who could take or leave a congregation according to my developing tastes and beliefs.

The Creed and Dr. Douglass

It has occurred to me, sitting in church, that we never know how many of the people beside us or around us—or before us, if we are the ministers—are feeling restless about the particular church they are in and wondering whether it is they or the church itself that is at fault for their uneasiness, for the fact that their minds wander so easily from what is happening to other things, such as the pot roast in the oven, the applications lying on the desk at work, the way their marriages are no longer exciting, the fact that little Josie needs braces and there is no money to pay for them.

Few people ever voice this uneasiness. They may assume it is only a passing whim, or that everyone feels it from time to time, so the best thing is to wait it out, not to give it a definite shape and articulation. They probably seldom identify it as the root of their problem, in middle life or growing senescence, the thing that's letting them down so they don't feel excited about life any more, don't greet each day with happiness as they once did, and don't feel a spring in their step as they go about their ordinary business.

In all my years in ministry, I can remember only one parishioner who ever spoke with me about having grown beyond a concept or practice in his church and passing through a period of questioning, a burgeoning dissatisfaction, that might one day compel him to leave that church.

It was in the First Presbyterian Church of Lynchburg, Virginia.

The parishioner's name was Dr. Courtney Douglass.

A tall, slender, slightly stooped, elderly man who might have resembled a disgruntled character in a Dickens novel, Dr. Douglass and his bride Ruth had gone off to China as medical missionaries a few months before World War II broke out and they were compelled to return to the U.S. They had continued their practice in Virginia, but apparently he had always felt traumatically interrupted by the war, so that he remained perpetually ill at ease with life. He and Ruth didn't have many friends. She was already showing signs of Alzheimer's when I arrived in Lynchburg, so that before long Dr. Douglass was attending the early worship service on Sundays and then returning home to care for her.

One Sunday I noticed that as others were saying the Apostles' Creed he was standing mute, clutching the pew in front of him and staring ahead with clenched jaws. I continued to track this for several Sundays and saw that it was his pattern. I'm not sure if some silent communication passed between us, but it wasn't long after I first noticed that he came to my office one day for a serious conversation about it.

"You've probably observed that I don't say the creed," he began.

I smiled and waited.

"I thought we should talk about it," he said. "I don't believe everything in it."

I smiled again, and told him it reminded me of a story one of my teachers, Dr. George Buttrick, told about himself when he was Preacher to the University at Harvard. As chaplain to one of the most secular universities in the world, and one that received some of the world's brightest young scholars, Buttrick was often accosted by students, and sometimes faculty as well, who brandished their agnosticism or outright atheism as a sword. It had happened so frequently that Buttrick developed a standard manner of responding. When a student burst into his office declaring "I don't believe in God"—an almost invariable opening gambit—his first move was to reach calmly for the humidor of cigars on his credenza and offer the student a smoke. Then he would perch on the edge of his big desk, his arms folded comfortably across his chest, smile ingenuously, and say, "Tell me about this God you don't believe in. Maybe I don't believe in him either!"

Dr. Douglass didn't crack a smile.

But then, I realized, he wouldn't.

"It's the part about descending into hell," he continued.

The creed, describing the suffering, death, and resurrection of Jesus, usually includes the phrase, between the death and resurrection, "He descended into hell." Some churches omit the phrase as being of dubious origin, but there was a strong medieval tradition, based on an obscure biblical text, that pictured Jesus, during the three days he was in the grave, as "harrowing the gates of hell," setting free innumerable souls immured by the devil.

I thought about how many other things we recited in the creed that might have given a scientifically-oriented man like Dr. Douglass some grief as well—the part about Jesus's being "conceived by the Holy Ghost," for example, or "the resurrection of the body and the life everlasting."

But he had fastened on the descent into hell, and it stuck like an intransigent fishbone in his throat so that he couldn't bring himself to utter the creed at all.

I volunteered that I considered the creeds of the church to be mere poetic statements—*mytho*poetic, in fact—not intended to be caviled over as if they were items in a case at law. In the beginning, I recalled, they had been intended to be sung, not said, the way we sing the great hymns of the church. They were, in other words, vast collective expressions of the general beliefs of Christians and not mere statements of fact to be quibbled over.

The word *credo*, in Latin, didn't mean precisely "I believe" but something more like "I *dare* to believe," almost in the category of *Credo quia absurdum est,* "I believe because it is absurd."

Dr. Douglass's taut, lined old face was impassive.

"I've seen too much to be flippant when I come to worship," he finally said. And he talked about things his eyes had beheld—people dying of all kinds of diseases, citizens put to death because they wouldn't accept their government's mandates, his wife's growing distemper of the mind.

"And while we're at it," he said, "I don't say the Confession of Sin either."

Presbyterians are very fond of the classical statement of personal sin and unworthiness they rescued from the Anglican Book of Common Prayer when they rejected Anglicanism as a whole:

> Almighty and most merciful Father, we have erred, and strayed from thy ways like lost sheep. We have followed too much the devices and desires of our own hearts. We have offended against thy holy laws. We have left undone those things which we ought to have done, and we have done those things which we ought not to have done, and there is no health in us. But thou, O Lord, have mercy upon us, miserable offenders. Spare thou those, O God, who confess their faults. Restore thou those who are penitent, according to thy promises declared unto mankind in Christ Jesus our Lord. And grant, O most merciful Father, for his sake, that we may hereafter live a godly, righteous, and sober life, to the glory of thy holy name. Amen.

I smiled again, because I didn't particularly like that bit of liturgical gloominess myself. I had always admired its grandeur of language and lilt of cadence. It does come trippingly off the tongue. But I often wondered if it really came from the heart when uttered by most modern worshipers.

The truth is that it simply suits the greater pattern of Calvinism informing the Presbyterian faith in general. John Calvin was a dour man whose theology exulted in the glorification of God and the total humiliation of humankind. His bleak assessment of human potential provided a fitting backdrop for the austere old Scots of the sixteenth century, perhaps, and the stern, implacable Puritans of the century after that, but it did seem to me a bit misplaced in the sunnier climes of modern life in America. "Calvin," I have often said half-jokingly, "was right: people are no damn good!" That was his total estimate of humanity, that we are unworthy to live, from the very get-go, because we have the rebellious seed of Adam in us, and even little babies cooing and clucking in their prams deserve, apart from the atoning blood of Christ, nothing but damnation.

It was easier for me to agree with Dr. Douglass on this one.

"I'll tell you what," I finally said. "I take seriously what you are saying. You have a right to feel comfortable in worship, as other worshipers do. Let me see what I can do to repair things a little for you. Not every Sunday, mind you. We can't jerk the rug out from under everybody else so suddenly. But part of the time—maybe part of the time it will be all right."

I began, authorized by no more than my conversation with Dr. Douglass about his unhappiness with parts of the service, to tinker with the liturgy. Not, as I promised, every Sunday, because I didn't want to unsettle those for whom the standard recitations were important, perhaps even a bulwark against the sense of total change and chaos in the greater world. But one Sunday a month, two Sundays a month, whenever it seemed to fit the mood of a particular service.

I kept the Confession of Sin in the liturgy, but often altered it from the old prayer we had once spoken to something like this:

> Ever-loving God, who knows the secrets of our hearts even when they are a puzzle to us, we admit to you the problems of our natures. We are seldom satisfied with what we have in life. We long for what others have, though we would soon become bored with it if it were ours. We do not realize our real worth and would like to be admired and famous. We often miss the simple gifts of every day because we are searching for what we do not have. Teach us to wait before you in prayer. Open our eyes and ears to the beauty and mystery of what is ours. Give us wholeness in your kingdom, through Jesus Christ our Lord. Amen.[4]

As for the creedal statement, I began alternating the Apostles' Creed with more contemporary assertions such as this:

4. Killinger, *Enter Every Trembling Heart*, 51.

I believe in God, who created the world and is still creating.
I believe that God is the God of time—of the slender moments
    that slip through the hourglass
    and of all the incomprehensible eons that constitute eternity.
I believe that God has given us the years of our lives
    as a period of growth and testing,
    to prove ourselves more worthy of the life to come.
God does not measure worthiness as we do,
    in terms of wealth and power and the observance
        of niggling rules;
    but God measures it in terms of love and grace and generosity,
    and whether we have thankful spirits that recognize the gifts
        laid daily at our humble doorsteps.
I believe the gifts are there, and that I must learn to see,
    and seeing, to respond;
    for it moves me that the Creator of the world
        would offer gifts to me.
If God has time for me, then I must make time for God.
    Amen.[5]

Apparently this arrangement satisfied Dr. Douglass. He still did not join in the saying of the creed (I couldn't see, because my eyes were closed, if he recited the Confession of Sin), but he told me once when I was visiting him and Ruth in their home that he was more comfortable with the liturgy than he had been.

"It seems more in keeping with the times we live in," he said.

But even though Dr. Douglass was the only parishioner I ever had who actually spoke to me about having outgrown the way we worshiped, he was probably the stormy petrel who represented many others who felt as he did. We live in an era of rapid transition when it is very difficult to find communal statements of faith as satisfying as the old ones were to former generations.

Before, people usually felt comfortable in their communities of faith. Entering church was like putting their feet into a pair of

5. Killinger, *Lost in Wonder, Love, and Praise*, 48–49.

old house slippers. Now it is difficult to strike a consensus on anything, even in the smallest group. The days when one size fitted
all are gone.

Sensitive pastors are mindful of this when they compose
prayers and sermons, and will take care not to exacerbate wounds
or create unnecessary tension in their congregations. But they
cannot help thinking, as they look into the faces of their congregations, that there are many people out there—rebellious teenag-
ers, distraught parents, miserable spouses, closet homosexuals,
people who have failed socially or economically—for whom the
patterns of liturgy, the words of the preacher, the whole attitude
and program of the church, are simply not meeting their needs,
so that they are wondering if there is any point in continuing a
meager relationship where they are or if they should move on and
try to make a connection elsewhere.

This is precisely what many of the leavers Brian Sanders, Julia
Duin, and others have written about have faced, and why many of
them decided to go. Fundamentalist and evangelical churches are
least prone to "temper the wind to the shorn lamb," but operate
under an unspoken mandate to exhibit their doctrines at every
opportunity and let the chips fall where they may. For this reason, the exodus from modern churches may be heavier from their
congregations than elsewhere. But my pastoral heart says this is
a good time both culturally and theologically to try to accom-
modate as wide a variety of personalities and outlooks as possible.

Singing Our Heresies

Recalling Dr. Douglass's problem with the Confession of Sin and
the Apostles' Creed reminds me of another way I grew away from
my old home church, and that was in its hymnody. When I was
growing up, I used to love the *Baptist Hymnal*, and sang its great
old hymns as lustily as if I had written them myself. I also thrived

on the Sunday night "Singspiration" hours after worship, when we all belted out chorus after chorus until we were hoarse from singing.

But as I studied the history of religion and understood how theologies had evolved and been transformed through the years, I began to feel a sense of discomfort intruding on my appreciation of those old hymns and choruses. "Blessed assurance," I had once sung with passion, "Jesus is mine!" But was he really, I began to ask myself? How patronizing that seemed, to call the Lord of faith, who lived twenty centuries in the past, *mine*. What right did I have to sing such words? How did I know he was mine? It seemed not only patronizing but narcissistic!

"Are You Washed in the Blood?" was another old hymn that troubled me. "Are you washed," asked the chorus, "are you washed, are you washed in the blood of the Lamb?" I had once sung those words with a kind of hypnotic adoration. Now I began to think, "How utterly gory!"

I knew the whole business was symbolic, that it referred to the Hebraic temple cult and the slaying of lambs for the sins of the people, and, once, on a mountain outside of Jerusalem, I had stood in the crowd on Passover and watched as a lamb was slaughtered and young Jewish boys tossed the bloody entrails among themselves with the ecstasy of children throwing a ball. But the words had begun to make me feel queasy and uncomfortable, so that I had to stop singing them.

The same was true for one of my all-time favorite hymns as a teenager, "The Old Rugged Cross."

> On a hill far away stood an old rugged cross,
>   the emblem of suff'ring and shame,
> And I love that old cross, where the dearest and best
>   for a world of lost sinners was slain.
> So I'll cherish the old rugged cross,
>   till my burdens at last I lay down.

> I will cling to the old rugged cross
> and exchange it some day for a crown.

When I was young, those words seemed winsome and gripping, and my heart swelled with devotion as I sang them, the way I'm sure the hearts of other worshipers did. But as I matured in my faith and realized that the theology of the Incarnation had to do with a lot more than Jesus's death on the cross—with a clash of ideologies and a commitment to the poor and outcast, and a lot of other things—I began to feel simplistic and idolatrous when I sang them.

"In the church, we are very careful not to speak or write heretical things," said my old mentor, the great Lutheran preacher Paul E. Scherer, "but we *sing* more heresies than you can shake a stick at!"

He was right. The tunes and rhymes induce a kind of mental somnolence in us, so that we don't pay attention to whether the words are literally true, and often they aren't.

I *miss* the glorious old hymns I once loved. I really do. So does my wife, who is far more musical than I. We both find as we grow older that we are humming or singing snatches of hymns and choruses from our youth, and trying to recall the exact words of them. They still have a slightly magical or intoxicating effect on our spirits. But we are both aware of a jarring disconnection between them and our present sense of theology, for which there has never been a correspondingly great and thrilling hymnody.

In recent years we have attended both Lutheran and Episcopalian churches occasionally, but have never quite got used to either because we frankly don't feel happy with their hymnody. The words and tunes don't embrace one another with the same appropriateness and even inevitability achieved by such great evangelical composers as Charles Wesley, Isaac Watts, and Fanny Crosby. Instead, they often clatter along like a load of lumber with the boards poking out at odd angles, so that they are barely sing-able, if at all.

A few contemporary writers have achieved a wonderful mar-riage of words and music. Brian Wren, Fred Kaan, Jane Marshall, and Natalie Sleeth come easily to mind. Still, it is the evangelicals and conservatives who do the best job with music. The more lib-eral or progressive wing of the church can't hold a candle to them.

In some ways, it isn't fun or easy to grow up and older. It would conceivably be nice to remain children all our lives, and play the games that used to give us such pleasure—Hide and Seek, King on the Hill, Red Rover, Hopscotch, and Tag—but that would be unnatural. All things proceed through a cycle of growth and change—even our religious faith.

This is why we outgrow the churches we knew—or some of us do. We wonder about those who don't appear to outgrow theirs, who seem able to remain as they were, to believe what they did, to frame everything in the same simple words that once served them, to still sing the same old hymns as lustily as ever and not feel a distancing of spirit, a disconnection of attitude, stealing over them like a fog from some abysmal swamp.

Maybe they're the lucky ones. Or maybe they just can't look unpleasantness in the face. Maybe they endure the disconnection with a certain stoicism of soul, the way people hang onto bad marriages or punishing situations of any kind. And, if they do, who's to judge them? One thing we all know, life isn't easy and we shouldn't badmouth those who act and feel differently from ourselves.

I don't like being suspicious of lyrics the way I am now. Sing-ing religious songs was easier and more enjoyable in my youth, when I wasn't so critical. But maturity does carry certain respon-sibilities, including one to speak truthfully of God and faith and service, and not to knowingly perpetuate lyrical heresies. Now I seldom sing lustily. And I admit that I rarely shed tears as I'm singing or feel like rededicating my life to God, something I did periodically in my youth.

I noticed that my wife and I weren't ashamed to sing the old songs when we were alone but would have been very reluctant to do so with a congregation at worship. Why was that? I think it was because we would not wish to endorse the theological opinions embodied in the old hymns and choruses. That would have seemed like a betrayal of everything we had struggled to learn and understand and fight for ever since we used to sing them. It would abrogate the distance we had traveled in our journeys, the battles we had waged and won in our own minds, the achievements we had made in forging a faith that was ours and that represented the best thinking and truest worship we could offer to God.

It would have been hypocritical of us to retreat to earlier stages of our development and repeat the words, sayings, and beliefs of those stages as if we still accepted them, when we didn't.

So there are no two ways about it. We simply cannot take up residence again today in the forms that once housed and expressed our youthful faith. We may sometimes feel homeless because we cannot do it, but now there is nowhere for us to go but forward. Life doesn't turn back upon itself. It must be lived in the only direction there is.

2

Outgrowing a Denomination

Baptists believe the errors in the Bible
were put there by God.

—ROBERT FLYNN, *GROWING UP A SULLEN BAPTIST*[1]

[At Moody Bible Institute we were taught
that] the Bible is the inerrant word of God. It
contains no mistakes. . . . For me, it was an
enormous "step up" from the milquetoast view
of the Bible I had had as a socializing
Episcopalian in my younger youth.

—BART EHRMAN, *MISQUOTING JESUS*[2]

Bumper sticker on a Unitarian's car: "I am still looking."

—HARVEY COX, *MANY MANSIONS*[3]

---

1. Flynn, *Growing Up a Sullen Baptist*, 9.

2. Ehrman, *Misquoting Jesus*, 4.

3. Cox, *Many Mansions*, 121. Cox cites this as a discovery made by his friend Krister Stendhal, Dean of Harvard Divinity School and Bishop of Sweden, who added that he thought of pasting a sticker on his own car saying, "We never lost it."

I was surprised, when I arrived at Harvard Divinity School, to learn that one-sixth of my new classmates were Nazarenes. Until then, I had thought of the Church of the Nazarene as a third-tier, back-of-the-bus denomination. But the young men with whom I went to school—there wasn't a woman in the class, as far as I knew—were attractive, personable, and first-class students. And all but one were in the process of transferring out of their denomination to become Presbyterians, Congregationalists, and Methodists.

As I came to know them—especially Darrell Holland and Harry Romeril—I learned that they had reached the tipping point with their denomination when they were students at Nazarene Theological Seminary in Kansas City. One of their professors, claiming the benefit of the Nazarene doctrine of "sinless perfection"—insisted that he had not sinned in more than ten years. It was more than these men could take. They said they felt somehow "embarrassed" by such a doctrine and by this professor's boast. It was a signal for them to move on to more congenial relationships.

I wasn't as prompt or decisive as they were. I don't think, at that point, that I'd had an inkling of a motivation to leave the Southern Baptist denomination I had grown up in. But what these Nazarenes had done began to make me aware of reasons for forsaking the denomination of one's origin, so that across the years I have made mental notes on quite a number:

> Embarrassment at a particular doctrine or doctrines in one's former denomination
>
> Embarrassment at a particular ritual or rituals in one's former denomination
>
> Embarrassment at the general impression given by one's former denomination
>
> Unhappiness with former denomination's emphasis on evangelism
>
> Unhappiness with former denomination's lack of emphasis on evangelism

Weariness with wrangling over certain issues, such as abortion, homosexuality, women in ministry, women in the diaconate

Excess moralism of former denomination

Lack of moralism in former denomination

Former denomination too large (e.g., Southern Baptists, United Methodists)

Former denomination too small (e.g., Disciples of Christ, National Association of Congregational Christian Churches)

Former denomination's theology too liberal

Former denomination's theology too conservative

Uncomfortable with former denomination's Sunday school literature

Former denomination too controlling over individual churches

Former denomination not controlling enough

Dislike or disapproval of former denomination's leaders

Scandal in former denomination's leadership or financial management

Former denomination too wealthy or self-serving

Unpopularity of a particular act or pronouncement of former denomination (e.g., Presbyterians' support of activist Angela Davis, Episcopalians' selection of a homosexual bishop)

Unconsciously drifting into another denomination by joining a preferred local church of that denomination

Conscious search for what seemed to be the best denomination

In previous times, people seldom changed denominations. We heard such phrases as "Once a Baptist, always a Baptist" and "Born a Methodist, die a Methodist."

But now there is tremendous fluidity among denominations, primarily for five reasons:

(1) Most denominations are no longer as distinctive as they once were.

(2) The population itself is more mobile, and people tend to "shop around" when they move to a new location.

(3) There is no longer a stigma attached to changing.

(4) There is no longer so much familial pressure to remain in a particular denomination.

(5) People today are accustomed to shopping for what they like
    best in everything, from houses and automobiles to schools
    and churches.

Within a culture of mobility, it is natural for people to ask themselves whether they have outgrown a particular denomination
and are ready to move on to another denomination whose doctrines, rituals, and sociological emphases are more compatible
with where they are in their own thinking.

My friends at Harvard were in advance of their times—that
was half a century ago—and making the choices they made would
seem much less dramatic today than it did then. When I have
asked new members in churches I pastored why they were willing
to transfer out of former denominations, they have said a variety
of things:

"I no longer believe in hellfire and damnation."

"I didn't like always having an invitation hymn at the end of
the service and feeling that pressure was put on people to come
forward."

"I didn't like their constant emphasis on giving money for
one cause or another."

"This church is more conveniently located for me, and I figure the 'brand' doesn't really matter all that much."

"The leaders in that denomination were too predictably conservative on moral, social, and theological issues."

Sometimes people switch denominations not because they
have changed but because they perceive that their denominations
have. In recent years, many members have left mainline Protestant denominations, especially the Presbyterian (USA), Episcopal, and United Methodist churches, because they believed their
denominations had become too liberal, especially in the interpretation of scripture and the issue of science versus religion, and
too tolerant on such moral issues as abortion and homosexuality.
There have been conservative rebellions in the midst of most of

the major denominations, and these have had a reverse effect on the more liberal members within those groups, causing them to leave for the United Church of Christ or Unitarian-Universalist denominations.

Is a person who tries to resist cultural changes by uniting with a more conservative denomination or group within a denomination simply resistant to growth, while those who join more liberal denominations or groups are actually demonstrating personal growth and development? I'm sure that would be a faulty assumption.

Take Thomas Oden, the noted Christian writer and theologian, for example. When I first met Tom years ago, he was a radical young professor at St. Paul's United Methodist Seminary in Kansas City. I was struck at the time by the way he took what I thought were rather extreme positions on both social and theological questions. But years later, when he had become a professor at Drew Theological School of Theology and I ran into him again, I was shocked at the transformation I saw in him. Conventionally clad and very serious in his demeanor, he was devoting his time and intellect to recovering and restating the ideas of the early church fathers, and had become as theologically reactionary as anyone I knew.

Contrary to the possibility that Oden had fallen into retrograde attitudes toward life and theology, I suspect he was discovering depths of meaning and understanding in the church fathers that could well have great significance for the entire field of theology in our time. We are too prone to dismiss those ancient figures for lacking the insights and historical advantage of our own culture, when in fact many were not only remarkably learned but possessed riches of devotion and imagination often missing on the contemporary scene.

Perhaps Oden really *grew* into who he had become and his interest in patristics represented a true *advance* in his personal journey for Christ. Certainly I would not judge his transformation as negative or backward in any way, but would prefer to regard this surprising turn in his life as a caution to any who would too quickly dismiss or denigrate the movement of any modern figure toward a more conservative position. Notable figures occasionally shock us by joining the Roman Catholic Church—think John Henry Newman and T. S. Eliot—so why should it surprise us that some people of intellectual substance actually move toward greater conservatism within the Protestant ranks?

Real growth is measured not by distance but by much subtler, more personal measurements. It may carry some people toward conservative positions and others toward liberal persuasions. Life is very complex, and some of the things we do may make perfect sense to us while appearing strange or senseless to others. My point is that people often outgrow their former denominations in various ways, and it isn't always possible to chart their growth by observing the direction in which it takes them.

Upward Mobility?

As a former Baptist myself, I have been interested to observe over the years how many Baptists who feel that they have outgrown the Baptist denomination end up uniting with the Episcopal Church.

There are several reasons for this, as I see it.

First, there is the matter of social status. Episcopalians are usually viewed as belonging at or near the top of the social ladder, while Baptists are among the denominations consigned to the lower rungs.

Second, Baptists seeking to align themselves with a church identified as more thoughtful and cultured usually believe they could not do better than become Episcopalians. Most Baptist ministers who have become Episcopalians are among the more reasonable, studious ministers I know.

Third, Baptists wishing to leave behind their evangelical backgrounds—particularly those embarrassing invitational hymns—often flee to the ritualism of the Episcopal Church, where members normally appear somewhat reserved and blasé about the forms by which they worship God.

Baptist pastors who become Episcopalians often outstrip other priests in their enthusiasm for bowing and scraping. I remember one such pastor at a large Episcopal church in Tyler, Texas, where I was a guest preacher for several days. Every time he passed the chancel, even at a distance of several yards, he paused to make a deep bow in the direction of the altar. It wasn't a perfunctory nod of the sort most priests get in the habit of offering, but a deliberately slow, demonstrative genuflection, as if he were still attempting to prove to the congregation that he was thoroughly converted to their religion.

It was about this time that a popular songwriter composed a ditty about ministers who become priests in the Episcopal Church. I don't remember the verses, but they began slowly and proceeded sedately until they reached the chorus. Then the music became suddenly frantic, a kind of high-pitched rock-and-roll, and the single word repeated over and over was "GEN-U-FLECT, GEN-U-FLECT, GEN-U-FLECT!"

The rector in Tyler might easily have been the model for such a song.

One of the most famous converts from the Baptist ranks into the Episcopalian priesthood was John Claypool, who had been one of the most respected pastors in the Southern Baptist Convention. While still a young man, John became senior minister of Crescent Hill Baptist Church in Louisville, adjacent to the campus of Southern Baptist Theological Seminary, where he preached regularly to many faculty members as well as hordes of future ministers. His sermons, always thoughtful and well-crafted, were distributed across the entire denomination.

The story of John's pilgrimage is interesting. While he was at Crescent Hill, he and his wife lost their small daughter to leukemia. During her illness, John preached an arresting series of sermons about his personal reflections on faith and suffering that was later published as *Tracks of a Fellow Struggler*. His wife sometimes complained that he did his grieving in the public arena, while she had to cope with hers alone.

From Louisville, John moved to Fort Worth, Texas, to become minister of the large Broadway Baptist Church. He continued to do excellent work there, and his reputation grew. But eventually he felt exhausted by the demands of such an immense congregation. I heard him remark that he felt like an old pump beside the road with a sign on it reading "Pump me!," that eventually became empty and incapable of producing any more water.

So he made a surprising move to a much smaller church, Northminster Baptist Church in Jackson, Mississippi. His marriage, which had been coming unraveled since the death of his daughter, ended. His wife returned to Texas to live with her mother, and he moved to New Orleans, where he received training as a pastoral counselor and underwent personal therapy.

From New Orleans, he went to Lubbock, Texas, where he became a member of the staff of Second Baptist Church, an unusually progressive Baptist church and one of the few that would consider having a divorced minister on its roster. And after a year at that church, he moved to Corpus Christi, Texas, under care of an Episcopal church while he studied for ordination as an Episcopal priest.

John married a woman from New Orleans and soon accepted an appointment as the rector of St. Luke's Episcopal Church in Birmingham, Alabama, a large, distinguished congregation in a well-to-do residential area of the city. There I reconnected with him—we had been at Baylor University together, our times had overlapped in Louisville, and I had preached for him in Fort

Worth—and we became part of a small support group that met weekly in the office of the provost of Samford University, where I had become part of the faculty.

John and I often met for lunch or coffee in Birmingham and talked about his move into Episcopalianism. I remember being startled by some of his admissions.

"I never felt comfortable as a Baptist," he said. "I always felt degraded by being the pastor of a Baptist congregation, because Baptists weren't as well educated or as socially prominent as Episcopalians. But the worst part was the worship. Baptists don't know how to worship. They want to be entertained when they come to church. They aren't really aware of God in the sanctuary; they want to visit with all their friends and then have a good time singing and listening to jokes from the pulpit. I always felt as if I was pandering to them, prostituting myself by coming down to their level of expectancy."

John once expressed the wish that he had gone to an Ivy League school instead of to a Baptist institution. He said he envied me for having had the courage to go to Harvard Divinity School. I reminded him that I had paid a price with the Baptists for not attending a Baptist seminary, but he brushed that aside, saying he would gladly have foregone the political advantages for a better education.

When I asked when his sentiments had begun to shift away from Baptist life and worship, he said it was the year he preached at the Southern Baptist Convention. It was during the war in Vietnam, and he felt spiritually burdened by America's involvement in such a contentious mission. Taking the parable of the Prodigal Son as his text, he suggested in his sermon that Vietnam was perhaps our nation's "foreign country" and that we would come back from the experience as the prodigal did, chastened and humbled. Many people who heard the sermon were critical of its anti-war spirit.

"I realized then," said John, "that most Southern Baptists have a herd mentality. They don't want to think about things intelligently or individually. If any of them dislikes something you say or do, then they all begin to dislike you. I began to dream of becoming an Episcopalian. I wanted to preach in a sanctuary with a divided pulpit and an altar, where people would acknowledge that God was at the center of their actions, not some guy in a pulpit telling them stories and trying to make them feel good."

"You know," he confessed at another time, "I don't think I ever knew how to worship until I became an Episcopalian. I could imagine doing it. I thought about what it would be like to lift the chalice in front of the altar and pray to God in behalf of my congregation. But I didn't think it would ever happen to me. I worried that I would die without experiencing true worship."

I can't imagine a more classic instance of someone's outgrowing his denomination. John was one of the most outstanding ministers in the Baptist tradition, a preacher who was the envy of 99 percent of the other ministers in his denomination, and he was ready to throw it over to become an Episcopalian, a rector in a church where few people knew him and some who did probably thought less of him because he had been a Baptist, and all because, over the years, he had grown out of the Baptist way of thinking and worshiping.

Leaving the Baptists

Like John, I too grew beyond the Baptists. But my situation was quite different. I have often said that I didn't leave the Baptists, they left me.

Because I believed that part of the genius of the Baptist faith was its cardinal support of the freedom of individual expression—Roger Williams, the first Baptist pastor in America, insisted on this, and thus made the Rhode Island colony a center of freedom of religion—I became distressed at the reppression of freedom in the Baptist Sunday School Board in Nashville, where I lived, and openly said so at a large student conference on the campus of Golden Gate Baptist Theological Seminary in Mill Valley, California, where I was the featured speaker.

I quickly learned that I wasn't free to speak my mind among Baptists. The president of the seminary, fearing reprisals from the Sunday School Board when it was time for the allocation of funds to his institution, followed me at the podium and spent ten minutes trying to rebut what I had said. He complained about me to the editor of the Baptist state paper in California, and the editor published a scurrilous editorial about me denouncing my beliefs and my morals. The executive secretary of the Sunday School Board joined in castigating me, and my engagements to speak at the Baptist assemblies in Ridgecrest, North Carolina, and Glorietta, New Mexico, that summer were both cancelled. Baptist universities and seminaries were told that they would lose their funding if I appeared as a speaker on their campuses. Employees of the Sunday School Board were warned that they would be fired if they were seen talking to me. Even our friends in the local Baptist church to which we belonged shied away from being seen with us.

Under interdiction, we left the Baptist church and became members of a Disciples of Christ congregation in Nashville. Later, we joined a small Presbyterian church where we had made some friends.

When I felt a midlife compulsion to return to parish ministry a few years later, I interviewed with churches all over the country without respect to denomination—a Baptist church in Houston, a Disciples church in Denver, a nondenominational church in Grand Rapids, a Congregational church in Los Angeles, and a Presbyterian church in Lynchburg, Virginia, to which I eventually accepted a call.

My virtual expulsion from the Southern Baptist fold—something of which I never dreamed at Harvard when my friends were enlisting in other churches—prepared me for openness to a wide array of denominational possibilities, and, in fact, for becoming a strong advocate of ecumenical experiences.

John Claypool once confessed to me that my leaving the Baptist church to become a Presbyterian was a major impetus in his thinking he could leave to become an Episcopalian, and that he often envied me for having the courage to go. There was an irony in this, for I had spent most of those years envying him for getting along with the Baptists and being able to stay!

How did I feel about leaving my original denomination?

I was often sad about it, even though I saw no alternative after I had been blackballed for any future with that denomination. For a while, I particularly missed the evangelical fervor of the Baptists. I often thought, as I considered my elegant and refined congregation in Lynchburg, that it would do them good to have to deal with an occasional altar call. I also wished we could use the Baptist hymnal, thinking that if we could only employ some of the fine old hymns of commitment in it they might light a fire of revival under all that elegance and refinement.

Both comments, about the fervor and the hymns, applied as well to my experience at the First Congregational Church of Los Angeles, where I went when I left Lynchburg. First Congregational was an unbelievably stately church. The huge sanctuary was modeled after the chapel at Magdalene College in Oxford, and the music was indisputably the finest in Los Angeles. But these conspired to serve a different purpose in worship from the one I hoped we could achieve, of molding the congregation into a true body of Christ and a loving, effective fellowship of believers.

Still, I grew a lot through my Lynchburg and Los Angeles experiences, so that when I went to Samford University in Birmingham as Distinguished Professor of Religion and Culture, hoping to pay something back to the Baptists for my rich initiation into the faith, I found Baptist religion unsatisfying in its shallowness and perfunctoriness. It needn't have been that way. The Baptist faith was once admirable for its insistence on the freedom of individual believers to think as they chose, to be fiercely independent of groupthink and ecclesial authority. Yet all around me I saw Baptist churches that were far from free, that were in fact enclaves of conservative robots, people who never voiced any thought or opinion different from everybody else's, as if they feared being caught out as different or heretical.

I had hoped Samford University might be different. It was, after all, a modern university, an institution with a public face, accountable to the public media as well as to the Baptists who controlled it. The president and provost were bright, competent administrators whom I had known for years and believed I could trust. If they wanted me on their faculty—I was the first of several "university professors" they employed to raise the level of scholarship in the faculty—then they would certainly protect my being there. They knew, going in, the price they might have to pay, for I had a reputation for honesty and outspokenness, which they said was one of the reasons they wanted me.

But even these administrators buckled under pressure from the conservatives who resented my presence there. When the dean of the university's divinity school, where I was based and had major responsibilities, deleted my profile and course offerings from the divinity computers and didn't assign me an office in the school's newly refurbished quarters, they didn't lift a hand to correct the situation. I was still free, they said uneasily, to teach in the English Department and the undergraduate Department of Religion.

I was ashamed—of them, of being on a campus where the Baptist ideal stood for so little, of myself for having believed things might be different and I could return to my roots. My roots had obviously never been what I thought they were. I had idealized them, had taken too seriously all the talk about intellectual and religious freedom among Baptists. They didn't really believe in the ideals of Roger Williams. They used him as an icon but weren't prepared to follow him as a saint. It was all a sham, and I was still a man without a denomination.

There was a painting on the wall of the dingy, unprepossessing office I was assigned after the divinity school moved off and left me. It was of a scapegoat, the shaggy, unfortunate beast described in the Old Testament as the bearer of the people's sins. It had a bloody spot on its head where the high priest had marked it with everybody's evil, and it had been driven into the wilderness, where supposedly it would be attacked by Azazel, the demonic spirit, and torn to pieces.

My first impulse was to remove the picture, for that poor, lonely creature standing forlorn in the desert had a particularly haunting look about it.

But then I realized our kinship, the goat's and mine, and I left it there, where I gradually became extremely fond of it. Some days, I actually talked to it about what we were both going through. I too was a kind of scapegoat, I told it, for I had been driven out by myself from the fellowship of the pure, of those who didn't wish to be tainted by my thoughts and speech.

Like the goat, I was abandoned to fend for myself against whatever demons inhabited the world around me.

I am still sad that my "experiment" of returning to the fold didn't pan out. No, it is more than that. I am sad that I have spent most of my adult life as an outcast, a foreigner, for no denomination takes you in completely when you have lost your welcome in another. Human nature is like that. I remember reading once about a man in Maine who had died in his nineties. His parents had brought him to the village where he lived when he was only two, and he had been there ever since. When he died, his fellow villagers, who respected him for his kindness, honesty, and industry, ordered a tombstone for his grave. It said: "He was almost like one of us."

Most people can move from denomination to denomination without much fuss. But I think it is different for ministers, whose fidelity to the denomination is part of their cachet.

Martin E. Marty, the venerable professor of church history at the University of Chicago, has often argued that denominationalism isn't dead, because, he says, it is needed. It arose out of differences of opinion about matters of faith, and at least some of those differences still exist.

That is true, to a limited extent. Certainly the differences continue to exist at the theoretical level. But they are no longer the differences that once evoked the various denominations. Originally, when Protestantism exploded onto the international scene in the sixteenth century, its varieties had to do with divergences in scriptural interpretation and the forms the various church groups should take. In the last half century, however, other fault lines have opened up that run right through the various denominations. They have to do with allegiance to an entirely new set of values and assertions that pit liberals against conservatives and individualists against conformists.

The churches that are thriving today aren't the old denominational churches at all, but the megachurches and metachurches that have foresworn denominational names and affiliation, which they rightly guessed were divisive and forbidding to potential members they wish to attract today. Most are aligned on the side of the conservatives and conformists, because liberalism and individualism don't readily attract a lot of people.

Their heroes are Rick Warren, Philip Yancey, Max Lucado, Joyce Meyer, Joel Osteen, Rob Bell, and a host of other young to middle-aged writers and speakers who are creating a new mythology about what it means to be Christian, combining the most sentimental materials from the old mythology with the tenets of motivational psychology to fashion a religion that promises success and comfort to all those from Baby Boomers on down who will buy into the sheen and glitter of its made-for-TV appeal.

In this bright new world of high-tech evangelism, denominationalism simply no longer has a place. It is passé, out of fashion, DOA. A few avid denominationalists don't yet know this, but as memberships decline and budgets nosedive and headquarters shrink they are bound to get the message. They are like all those moribund offices in the U.S. government that are never formally abolished but inevitably languish as their funding drops off beyond the point of sustaining them.

So, in a way, we have *all* outgrown denominationalism, regardless of how passionate a few people may remain about them. How many members do the Southern Baptists count, twelve or thirteen million? And the United Methodists, nine or ten million? They are the largest Protestant denominations in the country. Lump all the Protestants together and how many members can they count? Thirty million? Forty million? An *eighth* of the populace, in a country that thinks of itself as still being "very religious." Who are we kidding?

Ourselves, apparently.

3

Outgrowing Church, Period

The reign of God—the only reason for our
existence, the only purpose for church and our faith
life in general—is calling us to major concerns
beyond our own hierarchical structures of power.

—BARBARA FIAND, *FROM RELIGION BACK TO FAITH*[1]

A perfect storm of change is brewing over
America. . . . Like many of our Christian ancestors
we find ourselves in a moment when the faith is
changing drastically.

—GABE LYONS, *THE NEXT CHRISTIANS*[2]

Once upon a time the term "Christian" meant
wider horizons, a larger heart, minds set free, room
to move around. But these days "Christian" sounds
pinched, squeezed, narrow. Many people who identify
themselves as Christian seem to have leap-frogged
over life, short-circuited the adventure.

—PATRICK HENRY, *THE IRONIC CHRISTIAN'S COMPANION*[3]

1. Fiand, *From Religion Back to Faith*, 55.
2. Lyons, *The New Christians*, 19–21.
3. Henry, *The Ironic Christian's Companion*, 8.

Outgrowing church, *period,* is a radical thought, isn't it? Or is it? Perhaps that's what's happening to many people today. Now, in a time of globalization, perhaps church as the world once knew it is no longer necessary. Maybe it is time for it to become subsumed under something else that doesn't carry as much baggage as the church.

Because the church does carry a lot of baggage, doesn't it?

The Crusades.

The Inquisition.

Luther's war on the peasants.

Calvin and Servetus.

Cranmer, Latimer, and Ridley.

Cromwell's destruction of the monasteries.

The Puritans in New England.

Witch hunts.

Slavery.

Persecution of the Quakers and Mormons.

Segregation.

Acquiescence in Hitler's Germany.

The Moral Majority.

Attitudes toward homosexuality.

Sex scandals in both Catholic and Protestant camps.

Christopher Hitchens had good reason to give his book *God Is Not Great* the subtitle *How Religion Poisons Everything.*

As Helen Ellerbe says, "The Christian church has left a legacy, a world view, that permeates every aspect of Western society, both secular and religious. It is a legacy that fosters sexism, racism, the intolerance of difference, and the desecration of the natural environment."[4]

It is hardly an accident that there has been a spate of bestselling books condemning religion for its part in the world's miseries and atrocities. Hitchens's book. Richard Dawkins's *The God*

---

4. Ellerbe, *The Dark Side of Christian History,* 1.

Delusion. Sam Harris's *The End of Faith* and *Letter to a Christian Nation.* They are all flawed books,[5] but they are signs and portents. Signs that many people are ready to listen to such arguments. Portents that the era of the church may be approaching its end.

Would that be so unthinkable? What, after all, is so sacrosanct about church? It's leader died on a cross, didn't he? Why should the church continue beyond its time of fulfillment? John the Baptist said of Christ, "He must increase, but I must decrease" (John 3:30). Couldn't the same words be put into the mouth of the church, that the world's spirituality must increase but it must decrease?

The Apostle Paul said that the law, the Torah, was our *paidagogos,* our pedagogue or schoolmaster to bring us to Christ (Gal 3:24).[6] Suppose Christ and the church were further pedagogues to bring us to some kind of world religion. That is, what if they have done for us since Jesus's day what the Jewish law did until the birth of the Christian era?

Thirty years ago, I would have said this was foolish. Church will always be here. Jesus said the gates of hell wouldn't prevail against it. It must go on and on into eternity, seamless with the everlasting fellowship.

Now I am not so sure.

Now I think of the possibility of the church's transmogrification, its being alchemized into something so much greater, so much more spiritual, by losing its life in some kind of universal religious fellowship embracing Jews and Hindus and Muslims and Buddhists and naturists and totemists and everybody else. If

---

5. The learned Karen Armstrong says: "It is a pity that Dawkins, Hitchens, and Harris express themselves so intemperately, because some of their criticisms are valid. . . . But they refuse, on principle, to dialogue with theologians who are more representative of mainstream tradition. As a result, their analysis is disappointingly shallow, because it is based on such poor theology." (*The Case for God,* xvi.)

6. The NSRV translates the word "disciplinarian."

Jesus could die for the sins of the world, can't the church do the same? Can't it die even for its own sins? Can't it submit to some new world order in which its finest teachings—love, forgiveness, caring for the poor—are sublimated into new forms and codifications that everybody, literally *everybody*, can accept?

I would not have believed, fifty years or even twenty years ago, if someone had said to me that I would ever outgrow the church, that I would find it juvenile and immature in a world crying out for a higher order and a more refined spiritual understanding. No, I would have insisted, the church is the apotheosis of everything good and holy, it is God's design for the new world order, the heavenly kingdom.

But now, after a lifetime of working in churches, mingling with church members, and desperately trying to make silk purses out of sows' ears, I say I am not so sure.

Words are only semantical things, after all.

What does the word "church" actually mean? *Ecclesia*, in the Greek—"that which is called out." Jesus called disciples and commissioned them to carry the good news about God's salvation into the world. They did it, but not entirely without self-interest. They became Saint This and Saint That. They quarreled about places of honor. They left disciples who continued to quarrel and contend for control. Sometimes quarreling was all it was about—quarreling over position, quarreling over doctrines, quarreling over property, quarreling over leadership styles, quarreling over morality, quarreling over denominations, quarreling over quarrels.

Wouldn't it be nice to transcend all the quarreling? Merely to surrender it, to give it up in the face of a higher form of world religion?

I remember a friendly Jesuit I encountered once on a speaking trip. He was recollecting being at a conference of bishops in Paris following Vatican II. They were charged with redesigning the shape of the paten—no, not the paten, the cloth that is placed over it when the bread of the Eucharist is lying in it.

They were meeting in a comfortable hotel on the Left Bank. The room was warm and the discussions seemed interminable. Someone got up to open a window and let in some fresh air. But there was such a clatter going on in the streets below that they couldn't hear one another talk, so someone else got up and shut the window.

"Do you know what was going on in the streets below?" asked my Jesuit friend.

I shook my head.

"The Student Revolution," he said. "The university students were tearing up the cobblestones and throwing them at police in protest against the government and the way their tuition costs were rising.

"Imagine! The new world was being born outside our hotel—somewhat noisily, to be sure—and we were trying to redesign a piece of cloth for covering the goddamned paten!"

So I ask: Wouldn't it be nice to transcend all that, to permit the finest in Christianity to merge with the finest in Buddhism and Hinduism and Islam and become a truly first-class religion for the world of the coming centuries?

Of course it won't happen in my lifetime, and probably not in yours, whatever your age. But isn't it wonderful that it's coming, that it *will* happen, whatever we wish and however hard some of us try to defend things as they are? What were Captain Ahab's words about Moby Dick, "Will I, nill I, the ineffable thing has tied me to him; tows me with a cable I have no knife to cut"?[7]

We are bound to the future, whatever we may wish it to be, and we shall enter it whether we want to or not.

It is hard for ministers and priests to believe this. They are too lashed to the practical side of things, attempting to care for their

7. Herman Melville, *Moby-Dick*, 167.

parishes and preach the gospel and make sure nobody steals the altar cloths. "Of course the church will always be around," they insist. "It is sheer folly to think otherwise!"

But that is because they are so involved in making it work, in seeing that there is money to continue and people to fill the pews. They cannot really put themselves into the spirit of Philip Larkin's "Church-Going," the poem in which he describes stopping to look at a vacant church in the British countryside. Removing his ankle-clips and entering, he strolls up to the chancel and stands behind the great pulpit Bible. Surveying the empty pews, he wonders if the time is coming when women will steal up to the walls at night with sick infants and have them touch the stones for healing.

Yet this has already happened in many parts of Britain and Europe. There are churches as idle as the pagan altars that once dotted the roadsides of Guatemala and Costa Rica. "Time, like an ever-rolling tide . . ."

Please don't misread me. I don't have a vendetta against the church. I don't *want* it to disappear, to give way to some nameless, amorphous religion of the future. I am very happy with the here and now.

But the church's days are numbered, just the way those of the dinosaurs were, and the early wonders of the world—the Great Pyramid of Giza, the Hanging Gardens of Babylon, the Statue of Zeus at Olympia, the Temple of Artemis at Ephesus, the Mausoleum at Halicarnassus, the Colossus of Rhodes, and the Lighthouse of Alexandria—six out of seven of which have already disappeared.

A Play on Words

I imagine a play in the style of Eugene Ionesco, who wrote *The Chairs, Exit the King, Rhinoceros,* and other absurdist dramas. Perhaps it would be called *The Day the Church Disappeared* and would feature a conversation among a priest, a TV preacher, and a Tibetan monk:

> TV PREACHER: I don't know about you guys, but I'm hungry. Isn't there any food in this place?
>
> MONK: Only food for the soul, my brother.
>
> TV PREACHER: That's blasphemous!
>
> PRIEST: I don't think he meant it that way. Anyway, from the looks of you, it wouldn't hurt you to fast a little.
>
> TV PREACHER: Look who's talking! That's the pot calling the kettle black, if I ever heard it!
>
> PRIEST: No offense, son. But we're going to be here for a while, I think. Might as well get used to it.
>
> TV PREACHER: You, maybe. Not me. I've got souls to save, budgets to meet, books to sign, (*looking around*) promises to keep . . .
>
> MONK: Is it very demanding, being a minister on television?
>
> TV PREACHER: Damn right, it is! How do you think I keep my momentum going?
>
> PRIEST: Rome wasn't built in a day, son.
>
> TV PREACHER: No, but it was darned near destroyed in one!
>
> MONK: Things come, things go.
>
> TV PREACHER: Whaddya mean by that?!
>
> MONK: Nothing. I am only meditating.
>
> TV PREACHER: I wish you'd meditate somewhere else. You're getting on my nerves!
>
> PRIEST: It's possible we'll never get out, you know.
>
> TV PREACHER (*greatly agitated*): Whatddya mean, never get out?
>
> PRIEST: Nothing. Only what I said. We may be in this together for the duration.
>
> TV PREACHER: You, maybe, but not me! I've got things to do!
>
> MONK: Perhaps being is doing, my brother.
>
> TV PREACHER: What's that supposed to mean?! That sounds like a lotta crap to me!
>
> PRIEST: He's probably right, son. Anyway, this is a good time to find out.
>
> TV PREACHER: Whaddya mean, this is a good time to find out? It's *crap*, I tell you!

MONK: Maybe so, young man. But whatever it is, we're in it together. It is a good time to learn from one another.

TV PREACHER (*contemptuously*): Oh yeah? And what could I
learn from you, old man? How to study my navel?

PRIEST: You probably have a very interesting navel. Perhaps it is
worth some study.

TV PREACHER: Argh! You guys disgust me, you know that?!

(*Suddenly the TV Preacher grabs his heart, grimaces, and pitches
forward onto the floor. He twitches for a moment, then lies death-
ly still. The others merely regard him in silence before resuming
speaking.*)

PRIEST: What do you think we should do? Shall I give him last
rites?

MONK: Does it matter now?

PRIEST (*hesitating*): It used to. I'm not sure any more.

MONK: Do what you will. I am going to take a nap.

PRIEST: How can you sleep at a time like this?

MONK (*lying down and pulling his shawl over him*): This time,
another time. What is the difference?

PRIEST (*sitting down*): Perhaps you're right. It doesn't really matter, does it?

For those who insist on a point, it is this: we're all like the three
men in this little scene, shut up together in a shrinking world,
and there a sense in which the monk was right, being *is* actually
doing. What will be, will be, in spite of what we attempt to do
about it. We might as well relax, get along with one another, and,
if possible, even learn things from one another. Otherwise we'll be
like the TV preacher and do ourselves in from mere tension and
frustration.

Everything is in God's hands.

Ionesco, by the way, was a surrealist dramatist. He liked painting outrageous pictures that became *trompes d'oeil*, smiting his audiences with hard truths that were rendered no longer avoidable.

In *Exit the King*, for example, King Berenger (Ionesco called
most of his male characters Berenger) is watching his kingdom

collapse around him. Couriers bring news of disasters in the universe (the sun is dying, the Milky Way is curdling) and in his own realm (people are dying, no babies are being born, the sea is shrinking, rivers are drying up, the castle walls are crumbling). Preoccupied, he begins not to see the people in his own court, and as he ceases to see them they simply vanish into thin air.

At last, only he, his old wife, and his young mistress remain. Then the mistress disappears, and he is left alone with his wife. He slumps on the throne, weary from care and old age. His crown falls off and rolls away. His wife takes a gigantic pair of scissors and walks around him, severing the cords that bind him to this life. No longer useful, she disappears. He sits alone, a crumpled figure bathed in an eerie gray light. Then he disappears, and only the light is left. *Voilà*, exit the king!

What was Ionesco talking about? The death of royalty? The end of humanity? The surcease of everything?

Whatever it is, it is worth pondering with regard to the church. Word is arriving from everywhere that it is in trouble. Its walls are cracking and falling down. What was once vibrant and powerful is now suspect and tottering. Will the church go the way of Berenger's kingdom?

Does it matter?

Maybe the church will never die. Not if it manages to be the true church, the heavenly church, the one that is able to embrace and shelter all humanity under its wings.

But the church as we know it now—the church of most of our human experience—the church as seen by Hitchens and Harris and Dawkins—is hardly the heavenly church, is it?

Is it possible to outgrow the church, period, that is, to be a product of the church, to have loved it inordinately, to have given one's life to it in service, and yet to come to the point in one's pilgrimage where one says, "I can do without this now, I have learned to live without it, I am grateful for what it has provided

43

but now I am prepared to travel on without it, even as a crutch or a signpost"?

Talk about iconoclasm! That's what it's really about, isn't it? Tearing down idols.

I remember a little verse I copied onto the flyleaf of one my earliest Bibles, when I was a pimple-faced teenager:

> The dearest idol I have known,
> whate'er that idol be,
> Help me to tear it from the throne
> and worship only Thee.

That *is* what it's about, isn't it?

It's about being able to let the church go. It's about growing up and surrendering our need for church, depending only on God, *sans* church, *sans* preacher, *sans* Bible, *sans* everything. Even *sans* Jesus. For they are all only signposts indicating the way to go, and, when we have arrived, or are far enough along the road to know the rest of the way, we can give them up, trusting in God alone.

What was the old story evangelists once told, about the girl who felt the call to follow God, so that she packed a little valise and prepared to go into the world? "Do you really need all of that?" said a voice. So she put the things away and left the house bearing only a penny, which she clutched in her hand. Again she heard the voice: "Is your faith in the penny?" So she threw away the penny and continued down the road, singing.

Is our faith in the penny? In the church? In the Bible? In Jesus? In anything less than God, God's self?

You see?

I love Mary Rose O'Reilley's book *The Barn at the End of the World*. A Quaker who was raised as a Catholic, she now embraces all of life in its directness and immediacy. Fearful that she hasn't really been living—she is learning less and less from writers—she goes to live on a sheep farm for a year, and spends her time among the bawling, woolly-coated creatures, feeding them, nursing them, plunging her hand up their anuses to restore prolapsed rectums.

She does take a break, for a trip to England to visit a Sacred Harp singing festival—a convention for folks who treasure old shaped-note singing books, with triangles, circles, and squares instead of conventional modern notes. While there, she and her longtime male companion Robin prowl around an old Celtic church on the Welsh border, testing its acoustics and studying its carved figures. The figures remind her of ones she has seen among Guatemalan Indians. She thinks about primitive peoples and how they have lived without troubling over theology and questions of belief:

> British singers—confronted by the radical presence of Sacred Harp texts—will sometimes shyly ask if we're "believers," Robin and I. It's a hard question. Often, as soon as someone says, "I believe in God" or "I don't believe in God," I fear that I will not be able to talk deeply to that person. The fierce, unyielding word *believe* suggests—though not inevitably—that such a person views the issue within an analytical frame that is relatively meaningless to me. It is "believers" who so often take an uncompromising and fundamentalist position as though to defend the wheels and cogs and flysprings of their mental processes. Yet in the last few days people have opened their hearts to me with just this bashful phrase. Perhaps it is more an incantation than a theological query.
>
> Certainly I believe whatever I am singing for exactly as long as I'm singing it.[8]

I think I understand what she is saying—that the way people talk about belief or God or church is often cheapening. Seeking to pin down or reify these things has only the opposite effect, of banishing them from the moment's reality. Sometimes we honor them by not thinking about them, not speaking of them, not focusing on them too carefully, so that they can exist without our notice or verification.

8. O'Reilley, *The Barn at the End of the World*, 56.

Does that make sense? It does to me—for at least as long as I am thinking about it.

My wife and I saw a play by Jason Grote, called *2001*, at the Contemporary American Theater Festival in Shepherdstown, West Virginia. Grote employed the story of Scheherezade and the thousand and one nights as a basis for exploring many things, including Muslim-Christian relations after 9/11. The framework made many subplays possible. At one point, the famous Argentinian novelist, Jorge Luis Borges, made a cameo appearance to offer a thought about translations.

"Sometimes it is not translations that are unfaithful to the originals," he said, "but the originals that are unfaithful to the translations."

A fascinating statement. Does it apply to more than literature? Perhaps to everything that is, including religion and the church?

That is, is it possible that the church as we now imagine it, the church of the dreamers and theologians and great pastors, is actually *better* than the church of the New Testament itself, even though it is only a translation of the original? If we were able by some conjuring trick to return to the original church and experience it for a few hours, would we conclude that we really preferred the church of our own time?

I am quite serious.

What is the *reality* of the church? Not what it was at its inception, with the disciples, and not what it is now, in church councils and assemblies and local congregations, but the church *as God imagines it*. What does God want for the church? For it to protect itself, to safeguard its reputation and treasures, to preserve itself for all eternity? Or to fade into the edges of other world religions, to merge with Islamic and Buddhist and Hindu fellowships in order that it may leaven the loaf of all spirituality?

I contend that it is not being unfaithful to the church to outgrow it, to be able to leave it behind and continue our journey, armed with everything it has given us in the past.

Isn't this what parents expect of their children, not that the children will stay at home and honor them by waiting on them hand and foot, but by packing their bags and leaving home in order to make their way in the world with everything the parents have taught them and bestowed on them physically, morally, intellectually, and spiritually? It is unnatural to turn the home into a shrine and never leave it. And, similarly, it is unnatural for us to remain bound to the church, to spend the remainder of our lives slavishly trying to bolster it, to maintain it, to propagate it.

Outgrowing Church

The aim of every Christian, now that we understand our history and have an idea of what the future promises, should be to forsake the church and live for God without it, so that he or she is no longer fettered by it, dragging it along like a heavy weight that is bound to impede progress. Remember Paul's metaphor of the pedagogue or schoolmaster. What if Christ and the church are our college instructors to bring us to God?

All of this is undoubtedly frustrating to conservatives and fundamentalists, who are by now pulling out their hair over the radical and outlandish things I have been saying. But I challenge them to submit both our views to the judgment of posterity. It is disloyal to Christ and the church to speak of going beyond them only if their aim from the first was to glorify themselves and focus everyone's attention on them. But if, on the other hand, they regarded themselves as mere beacons in a dark and murky world to point people to the truth and help them focus on God as the loving and spiritual center of everything, then it is only right and proper, at some point, that every disciple be prepared to progress beyond our present understandings of Christ and the church to new and higher understandings that permit the unification of all God's creatures in a religion transcending all our former ones.

Only since I have been retired from active ministry and teaching have I been able to think this way. Before, I was too busily involved in the hand-to-mouth work of Christianity—teaching, preaching, giving pastoral care, marrying, burying, and baptizing—to turn my mind to such things. But now I am able to consider the matter with more detachment, the way an old general studies the battlefield after retiring from it.

I am frankly amazed at what I am feeling and seeing. It seems so clear to me now, after a lifetime of laboring in the church's vineyard, that the church must die—or we Christians must die to it—in order to usher in the kingdom of God Jesus was always talking about.

Our problem is language, and how we think about things. We absolutize the symbols, attributing to them the reality of things in themselves. As James P. Carse says in one of the remarkable essays in *Breakfast at the Victory*, we create distinctions where none exist. As Taoists, Buddhists, Sufis, and bookies all know, everything is in flux.

> Using words to isolate some portion of the flux is like taking a photograph of the surface of the ocean. No sooner does the lens close than a different ocean appears. It may be the same ocean but no single photograph, or any number of photographs, can capture its oneness. The truly real, as the Hindus say, is *neti neti*, not this and not that.[9]

We pride ourselves on language, Carse says, on being able to name things. Aristotle and Descartes both thought this a sign of our superiority to animals. But, mystically speaking, "the opposite is true: because the animal is closer to its own silence, it is closer to

---

9. Carse, *Breakfast at the Victory*, 24.

God."[10] Our very knowledge gets in our way and betrays us into trusting it too much. "Knowledge can lift the veil. It can also become the veil."[11]

In our case, talking about the church becomes a veil. Instead of bringing us closer to God, it actually removes us further from God. It becomes a distraction from God.

It isn't our business as servants of God to spend our time and energy attempting to preserve and build up the church. When we do that, we turn the church into an idol and actually frustrate the work of Christ to bring the world to God.

Years ago, the noted missiologist J. C. Hoekendyjk said in a book aptly named *The Church Inside Out* that we make a big mistake if we think that the order of things is GOD–CHURCH–WORLD, when in fact it is GOD–WORLD–CHURCH. That is, we are wrong to conceive of the church and its mission as some kind of intermediary between God and the world that God wanted to unite in divine love. By thinking that, we have made the church into something it was never intended to be, an object in itself. It is time, knowing what we know today, to explode that object, to destroy it in order to let God be God. The church is only a fellowship club for those who have met God in the secular order.

Nobody in the world has ever been more proprietary than some of the most successful leaders of the church. They have placed all God's property under their care, signed over all God's rights to themselves, and generally behaved as if they, not God, were in charge of everything. They strutted around the way Idi Amin strutted around Liberia, acting as if they were the sun, the moon, and the stars, and everybody ought to bow down when they passed.

We can only imagine what Jesus would say to the church if he were suddenly to appear today and see what a mess it has made of

10. Ibid.

11. Ibid., 30.

its opportunity to serve God. "You have scoured heaven and earth to increase the size of your organization," he might say, remembering a speech he once gave to the Pharisees, "and have made people twice the sons of hell they already were!"

Nikos Kazantzakis, the Nobel prize-winning author, berated himself in his autobiography *Report to Greco* for spending so much of his life thinking and writing about things instead of actually doing them. "You are a nanny goat, I frequently told my soul, trying to laugh lest I begin to wail. Yes, a nanny goat, poor old soul. You feel hungry, but instead of drinking wine and eating meat and bread, you take a sheet of white paper, inscribe the words wine, meat, bread on it, and then eat the paper."[12]

It is the same with most Christians. We worry our faith to death instead of absorbing it, celebrating it, and living it with all the stops pulled out. We anguish over our orthodoxy instead of being caught up in the Spirit of God. We patrol the borders of our theological property like Dobermans at a junkyard instead of embracing truth and beauty wherever we find it!

If heaven is anything like I imagine, it will have no walls, no boundaries, no demarcations of any kind. There won't be any signs reading "Hebrews Here," "Christians Here," "Muslims Here," or "Hindus Here." It will be like one giant reception hall where Sufis and Zen Buddhists and Mormons and Christian Scientists will do-si-do together to the music of a Zoroastrian rock band. And Moses and Jesus and Buddha and Mohammed will all have their heads together planning a birthday party for God, even though none of them can even guess how old she is!

12. Kazantzakis, *Report to Greco*, 190.

4

The Disconnect between Jesus and the Church

The test of worship is how far it makes us
more sensitive to "the beyond in our midst," to
the Christ in the hungry, the naked, the homeless
and the prisoner. Only if we are more likely to
recognize him there after attending an act of
worship is that worship Christian rather than
a piece of religiosity in Christian dress.

—JOHN A. T. ROBINSON, *HONEST TO GOD*[1]

My primary vision of Christ is that he is
a source of godly empowerment who calls me
beyond my boundaries.

—JOHN SHELBY SPONG, *A NEW CHRISTIANITY
FOR A NEW WORLD*[2]

A funny thing happened to me on the way to writing this
book. I flew from New York to Memphis, where I lectured
three times at the national gathering of the Cooperative Baptist

1. Robinson, *Honest to God*, 90.
2. Spong, *A New Christianity for a New World*, 148.

Fellowship, the large moderate group that broke off from the Southern Baptist Convention a few years ago. One of the lectures was called "A Reinterpretation of the Gospel of Mark." It was based on the research I had done for my book *Hidden Mark: Exploring Christianity's Heretical Gospel*.

In the Q and A following the lecture, someone asked a question about the Jesus of the four Gospels.

I could not afterwards recall my precise answer, but I'm sure I said something to the effect that the Jesus of the Synoptic Gospels was a much humbler figure than the Jesus of the Fourth Gospel. In Matthew, Mark, and Luke, he was a man led by the Holy Spirit and selected by God to be the Messiah because he was faithful and good. In the Gospel of John, written later than the other Gospels, after the church had had time to embellish its legend of the Savior, he was viewed as pre-existent with God and a co-creator of the world.

There happened to be a reporter present from the Southern Baptist Press in Nashville—part of the conservative denomination from which the Cooperative group had broken away. The following day, the front-page headline of the newsletter from that press declared, "CBF Speaker Denies the Deity of Christ."

Horrified at the impression such an announcement might create in their fellowship, the leaders of the CBF huddled and issued a strong counterattack on the press and its tactics. The various Baptist state papers picked up the story and made a big to-do about it. Bloggers began to argue about what I had or hadn't said. Everything was in confusion because the CBF would not release the recording of my actual comments. The controversy went on for weeks. Only once, in all the hubbub, did anyone contact me to ask what I had said. Unfortunately, I could not respond with complete accuracy because my remarks had been unscripted and I didn't have a record of them either.

The excitement occasioned by this very minor footnote in the history of religious conferences is probably a key to our modern uneasiness about the reliability of orthodox views of Jesus and the doctrine of the Incarnation. Was Jesus only a man chosen by God to be the Savior of the world, or was he the transcendent Christ of the Fourth Gospel? And did Jesus himself found the church or did the church invent the story in which he is pictured as establishing it upon the confession of Peter that he was the Christ? Conservatives are right to be worried, because everything connected with the beginnings of Christianity is now being called into question.

In *The Five Gospels: The Search for the Authentic Words of Jesus*, the summary of the findings of the famous Jesus Seminar, the words of Jesus to Peter in Matthew 16:18–19, "You are Peter, and on this rock I will build my church," were unanimously judged by the large panel of distinguished scholars—hundreds of them—to be a total fabrication by someone in the early church, possibly Matthew himself, for they reflected "Peter's position in Matthew's branch of the emerging Christian movement."[3]

Even Luke, who wrote the Gospel of Luke and the Book of Acts, the only history of the church in its beginnings, failed to mention this ceremonial statement. Its absence there, as in the other Synoptic Gospel, Mark, makes its appearance in Matthew even more suspect.

Few scholars question the fact that the church as a historical entity emerged from the Jesus movement of the first century, or that its charismatic genius somehow accrued from the story of his resurrection from the dead and the galvanizing effect this had on his little band of followers, with Peter as their leader.

Even in a religious milieu where strange sects and mystical cults were forever rising and falling like bubbles in a cauldron, the church's phenomenal spread throughout the Roman Empire was remarkable, and its eventual recognition by Constantine as the

3. Funk and Hoover, eds., *The Five Gospels*, 207.

state religion, nearly three centuries later, attests to its apparently miraculous power and genius.

Jaroslav Pelikan, the distinguished church historian at Yale, aptly began his stately volume, *Jesus Through the Centuries*, by reminding us that we have no actual photographs of Jesus—no incontrovertibly accurate records—but only portraits by various witnesses who saw him from their own personal vantage points, and that therefore we cannot say anything about him with absolute certainty. Not anything. Albert Schweitzer was correct when he ventured that each successive epoch has found its own thoughts in Jesus and recreated him according to its own character. Christian tradition had in fact developed before any Gospels were written, and therefore Pelikan found it necessary to caution his readers that "every later picture of Jesus is in fact not a picture based on an unretouched Gospel original, but a picture of what in the New Testament is already a picture."[4]

All of this is to say that any judgment about Jesus's relationship to the church at any point in the church's history is highly speculative, and depends largely on the critic's own picture of who Jesus really was, what he actually said, and, if he were physically present at the time, what he would think about the church's use of him then as its foremost icon.

To be fair, I should begin by stating as precisely as possible my own estimate of who Jesus was and what he intended. While I honor the church's lofty vision of him as the Universal Christ of John's Gospel—invariably, I think of Graham Sutherland's unique risen-Savior tapestry in the chancel of Coventry Cathedral and the magnificent mosaic of the Pantocrator Christ on the chancel ceiling of the Sacre Coeur in Paris—my own study of the Gospels leads me to conclude that Jesus in the flesh had no idea of a resurrection or extended ministry for himself. I agree with Robin Meyers, who says, "Claims of biblical infallibility are identical to

4. Pelikan, *Jesus Through the Centuries*, 10.

the claims of the metaphysical divinity of Jesus. Both make idols of the temporal, and idolatry is the mother and father of all sins."[5]

I regard Jesus as a limited, earthly player in one of the world's greatest dramas, who came onto the stage as a disciple of John the Baptist, inherited John's mantle, became an inspiring teacher of divine insights and (in Morton Smith's favorite term) a magician, and, in his stubborn loyalty to the truth, held out against the paranoiac scribes and Pharisees who controlled Israel's religious life until they finally pressured the Romans to put him to death.

Was he then raised from the dead?

Against all logic, I believe he was. If he wasn't, it certainly spoils a good story and a great deal of history.[6] To repeat that wonderful line from Borges, "Sometimes it isn't the translation that is unfaithful to the original, but the original that is unfaithful to the translation."

For me, the real portrait of Jesus's resurrection is not in Matthew or Luke or even John, but in Mark, especially in those dramatic accounts in Mark 4:35–41 and 6:45–52 of Jesus calming the sea. The reason I prefer Mark's version is that he places the resurrection effect, not in the final chapter with its truncated "authorized" version, but in those remarkable sea stories. I have no doubt they are both post-resurrection appearances.

In the first, Jesus is "asleep" in the boat with the disciples— the word Jesus used shortly afterward to describe a young girl, the daughter of the synagogue leader, who is plainly dead (Mark 5:35–43). In the second, he comes down from a mountain where he is praying and walks on the water to the nearly shipwrecked disciples. In both instances, Jesus rebukes the waves that threaten

5. Meyers, *Saving Jesus from the Church*, 29. Meyers says the claim that Jesus is God is "the dominant American heresy" (93).

6. As James D. G. Dunn says in *Did the First Christians Worship Jesus?*, "there can be little or no question that what the first Christians believed had happened to Jesus after his death transformed their appreciation of him completely. For they were convinced that God had raised him from the dead" (101).

the disciples, who represent the early church. The Jesus of these vignettes is the spiritual Christ whose presence sustains the ecclesial fellowship in its darkest hours.[7]

Were these happenings literally true?

I like Harold Pinter's statement in his 2005 Nobel prize acceptance speech: "There are no hard distinctions between what is real and what is unreal, nor between what is true and what is false. A thing is not necessarily either true or false; it can be both true and false."

But I would not vote for the literal truth of the sea passages. Instead, they are figurative stories, parables of the early church's experience. The church was often represented in iconography as existing in a ship at sea, and more than once its members believed themselves miraculously spared through the intervention of the Savior.

Does this mean that the resurrection itself was not literal, that it didn't actually occur? Not necessarily. I am not such a strict materialist as to believe that no strange or inexplicable things ever occur in the physical universe. On the contrary, I think they happen often—all the time—and we seldom behold them because we don't expect to see them.

Do I believe that Jesus lives today and presides over the heavenly kingdom, as the early Christians came to believe, at the right hand of God? I do not especially have a problem with that idea, but it isn't important to me because I have never felt a need for Jesus as an intermediary with God. The only time I had a life-changing encounter with a heavenly being, it wasn't with Jesus but with an angel. Consequently I never think of Jesus in the intercessor's role. Other Christians have reported visions of him—Betty Eadie describes one in her popular book *Embraced by the Light*—but I cannot personally corroborate such appearances.

---

7. For an extended discussion of this thought, see my *Hidden Mark*.

Having disclosed my beliefs, I am now ready to say some things about areas in which I see a major disjunction between Jesus and the life of the church in our time. Is that serious? I believe it is, because everybody speaks of Jesus as Lord of the church and therefore Lord of their individual lives. If he were truly the Lord, the relationship might be vastly different from the way I see it as existing now.

There are four primary areas in which I see the disjunction: (1) in the church's moralism, (2) in its materialism, (3) in its lack of courage, and (4) in its deficiency of love and compassion.

(1) The Church's Moralism

It is amazing, when you think about it, that the church ever got into the morality business at all.

Jesus didn't.

He laughed about the fact that some people called him "a drunkard and a glutton." He consorted with people who were, by accepted Jewish standards, immoral and unblessed. He often broke the sabbath law. And he sometimes instructed his disciples to disregard the strict rules governing personal hygiene before eating.

He did talk about morality, and reminded the *unco guid* or "uncommonly good," as Robert Burns called them, that there is a depth to real morality they hadn't begun to plumb. In the matter of adultery, he said that the person who has lusted in his heart has as good as committed it (Matt 5:27–28). Whoever is angry in his heart, he said, is as guilty as the person who murders (Matt 5:21–22). Almsgiving, a favorite way of cultivating good opinion, he condemned as useless before God unless done secretly, without personal advantage (Matt 6:1–4). Fasting and praying should likewise be done in secret (Matt 6:5–7, 16–18). Judging the motives or behavior of others was flatly repudiated, as most people tend to find a speck of dust in another's eye while missing the log in their own (Matt 7:1–5).

Yet despite these incisive observations in the Sermon on the Mount (in Matthew) and the Sermon on the Plain (in Luke), it is surprising how seldom Jesus was portrayed as a merchant of morality. On the contrary, the Gospels depict him as a man of lofty purpose and grand, decisive action who gave little thought to trivial matters of sin and morality and seldom called others into account for anything more than hypocrisy.

He ate freely with sinners and rode above the criticisms of him and his disciples as loose, nonobservant, and sinful. In a textually questionable but helpfully suggestive pericope in John 8:1–11, he refused to condemn an adulterous woman and reminded the men who had exposed her of their own sinful natures. Dying on the cross, he told the criminal crucified beside him, "Today you will be with me in Paradise" (Luke 23:43).

It is highly remarkable, therefore, that within only a few years of Jesus's death the church that sprang up around his memory had already developed a stringent code of morality. The book of James, believed by some to have been written by Jesus's own brother, warns believers against surrendering to temptation (1:12–16) and reminds them of the importance of good works to accompany their faith (2:14–17). They are to guard their tongues against idle talk (3:1–12) and avoid friendships with the world (4:1–4), lusting after money (5:1–6), grumbling about one another (5:9), and swearing oaths (5:12). First Peter urged readers to "abstain from the desires of the flesh," conduct themselves with honor among the Gentiles, "accept the authority of every human institution," and not to use their freedom "as a pretext for evil" (1 Pet 2:11–17).

The Apostle Paul, who probably did more to set the tone for the future of Christianity than any other individual, established a tenuous balance between Christ's work as Savior and the obligation of Christians to live moral, upright lives. His letters always recalled the munificence of divine grace, but they were also filled with exhortations to morality. *To the Thessalonians:* "abstain from fornication" (1 Thess 4:3), from wronging or exploiting brothers and sisters in the faith (1 Thess 4:6), from returning evil for evil (1 Thess 5:15), and instead "aspire to live quietly, to mind your own affairs, and to work with your hands (1 Thess 4:11). *To the Galatians:* avoid the "works of the flesh": "fornication, impurity, licentiousness, idolatry, sorcery, enmities, strife, jealousy, anger, quarrels, dissensions, factions, envy, drunkenness, carousing, and things like these" (Gal 5:19–21), because "God is not mocked, for you reap whatever you sow" (Gal 6:7). *To the Corinthians:* avoid quarrels and divisions (1 Cor 1:10–17), sexual immorality (1 Cor 5:1–8), and anyone who is "sexually immoral or greedy, or is an idolater, reviler, drunkard, or robber," driving that person away (1 Cor 5:9–13); don't eat food sacrificed to idols (1 Cor 8:1–13), eat and drink communion unworthily (1 Cor 11:17–22) or marry unbelievers (2 Cor 6:14–15). *And to the Romans:* don't curse your enemies (Rom 12:14), be haughty (Rom 12:16), or repay evil for evil (Rom 12:17); be subject to the governing authorities (Rom 13:1–4) and don't refuse to pay your taxes (Rom 13:6–7); keep the commandments (Rom 13:9–10); don't despise those who do not eat meat (Rom 14:1–4) or put stumbling blocks in front of the weak (Rom 14:13); and avoid anyone who teaches anything other than what you've already been taught (Rom 16:17–18).

It is easy to grant that most of the exhortations in early Christian writings were attempts to keep the members of the church in harmony with one another and to prevent their criticism by people outside the church. Nevertheless, the groundwork for a strong, often overweening Christian morality was laid, so that, in the years ahead, it frequently overshadowed the message of love and forgiveness taught by Christ.

By the time of Tertullian, in the early third century, this influential Christian legalist was saying in *De pudicitia* that, while

Christ can intercede for such "daily" sins as anger, swearing, lying, breaking promises, or even physical violence, "there are other sins very different from these, as being too serious and ruinous to receive pardon. Such are murder, idolatry, fraud, denial [of Christ], blasphemy, and of course, adultery and fornication, and any other violation of 'the temple of God.'"[8]

And Origen, often named the greatest theologian of the third century, set the stage for a medieval church that focused obsessively on individual sins and the church's management of forgiveness. In his commentary on Romans, he cited an obscure verse from the Septuagint, "No one is clean from sin, even if his life has only been for one day," then argued: "It is for this reason that the Church has received from the Apostles the tradition of giving baptism to infants. For they were entrusted with the secrets of the divine mysteries, and they knew that there were in all mankind innate stains of sin which had to be washed away by water and the Spirit."[9] Querulously, he argued in his *Homily on Leviticus* that our innate sins are the reason "you will never find any of the saints celebrating his birthday, or holding a birthday party; nor keeping his son's or daughter's birthday as an occasion of rejoicing. Only sinners celebrate birthdays with rejoicing."[10]

Thus the gracious, understanding way Jesus dealt with sin and sinners throughout his ministry, climaxing with his plea on the cross, "Father, forgive them, for they know not what they do," and Paul's delicate balance between grace and law, became lost in the medieval subtext of church law and doctrine, which was essentially as legalistic as the system Jesus died opposing.

Luther recovered the Pauline emphasis on grace for the Reformation, and, as conversations in his *Table Talk* make obvious, relished flouting conventional moralism in his personal life as well

8. Henry Bettenson, ed., *The Early Christian Fathers*, 213.

9. Ibid., 282.

10. Ibid., 283.

as in his theology. But the gains he and other Reformers made were essentially short-lived, for the Calvinists and even some of Luther's own successors turned out to be closet legalists, even while talking about grace and forgiveness, and most churches in subsequent centuries reverted to the petty moralism that is apparently endemic to the human brain.

Today, churches are almost invariably identified with excessive views on morality, and defined more by what they are against than by what they are for. In drama and literature, they are ridiculed for the prissiness of their clergy—or, if the clergy are not prissy, their excesses—and the hypocrisy of their moral standards, by which they behave precisely the way Jesus described the Pharisees as doing, straining at gnats and swallowing camels. Sinclair Lewis pilloried American Protestantism in *Elmer Gantry*, his story about a rake-hell Methodist minister who was as lacking in spirituality as a drug pusher on a grade-school playground. Graham Greene, a devout Catholic, did the same for Catholicism and its "whiskey priests" in *The Power and the Glory*. Churches are depicted, more often than not, as societies of moral pretenders filled with lust, greed, envy, and all the other deadly sins, and more afraid of others' finding them out than of the sins themselves.

Sam Harris, in *Letter to a Christian Nation*, accuses the church of allowing people "to imagine that their concerns are moral when they are highly immoral." By emphasizing certain moral issues and neglecting others, it manages to distort the whole moral spectrum. For example, he says, Christians "expend more 'moral' energy opposing abortion than fighting genocide." They are "more concerned about human embryos than about the lifesaving promise of stem-cell research." They "preach against condom use in sub-Saharan Africa while millions die from AIDS there each year." In their fear of sex in any form—an abiding preoccupation since Victorian times—they often oppose the very means of alleviating suffering in people with sexually transmitted diseases. For example, there is now a vaccine that has been proven almost 100 percent effective in HPV, the most common STD. But religiously conservative leaders in Washington have opposed its use on the grounds that they consider HPV a valuable disincentive to sexual promiscuity.[11]

What Harris is saying, in effect, is that Christians preach one thing—love of one's neighbor—and do exactly the opposite. It is hard to dispute that claim on the evidence we have seen since the times of Jesus. Christians have usually masked their fears, doubts, and hatred by saying that what they seek for others in their zeal for moral living is "for their own good," just as the Inquisition-ists of the Middle Ages and the Puritans in seventeenth-century New England claimed that their bitter efforts to extirpate personal freedom was for the sake of their victims.

As a pastor, I often witnessed this kind of duplicity in the congregations I served: secret drinkers who railed against strong drink, sexual purists who turned out to be adulterers or pedo-philes, wife abusers who resisted admitting homosexuals to church membership, guardians of the treasury who were stealing from their companies, pious realtors who opposed open housing, merchants who fiddled with expiration dates on food, publicity-seeking donors who rigged their gifts to get them back again after securing credit for them.

I think church members are on the average more loving, honest, truthful, and generous than the population at large. Many I have known have been morally exemplary and have not gone around blowing trumpets before their good deeds. But most of us are merely human, when the truth is told, and prone to faults. Goodness is not and never has been the church's strongest suit. All churches, under the microscope, have exhibited what A. O. Taylor, the great medievalist, said of the Roman Catholic Church in the Middle Ages, that it was a "spotted reality."

11. Harris, *Letter to a Christian Nation*, 24–26.

This is why I find a disconnect—and a very serious one—between Jesus and the church when it comes to morality. Jesus wasn't really about morality. He understood how tricky it can be as a means of judging others, or, for that matter, even of judging ourselves. He was therefore about grace and forgiveness, about loving others in spite of their behavior, about encouraging people to accept and embrace one another instead of accusing and convicting one another.

Having watched him in action in the Gospels, I can only say that if he were alive today he would live in a tenement house in the worst part of the city, fraternize with crack heads and prostitutes, wash the bedclothes of people with AIDS, and generally take the part of immigrants and outcasts. He might visit the lovely churches and cathedrals, and hang around university campuses and the halls of Congress, but that would not be his real milieu. His real milieu is wherever people are hurting and are most invisible to the rest of the world, which is going blithely on its way as if there were no real pain and suffering that merit its losing any sleep.

Jesus inverted morality to show us what it really is—to love his little ones and care for them as our own—and that is precisely what the church has failed to understand or practice.

(2) The Church's Materialism

In "The Leaver's Manifesto" at the end of Brian Sanders's *Life After Church,* there is a section called "Doing Justice." This is what it says:

> We dream of a church that takes a prophetic stand against all kinds of evil, not only spiritual but also societal. All sin and injustice is the enemy of the church and the kingdom of God. In word and in deed, the church has to begin with itself by confronting the sin of materialism and the hoarding of wealth at the expense of the poor.[12]

12. Sanders, *Life after Church,* 185.

In my lifetime, I have been the minister of eight churches. Five were small, insignificant parishes in the country or on the margins of cities. Three were prominent city congregations.

I never had any trouble feeling that the small churches were real havens from the secular world or that they were residences of Christ and his people. There was never enough money to keep the buildings in repair, but nobody minded. We weren't worried about architecture. What mattered was the fellowship, and the fact that we came there to put our arms around and encourage one another for our lives when we left there.

One was a simple frame building in a stand of poplar trees. Hence its name, Poplar Grove Baptist Church. It was a plain, unadorned rectangle about the size of a three-car garage. It was finished inside with tongue-and-groove boards and on the outside with simple white clapboard. There was an eight-foot concrete apron across the front of the building. Inside, there were four or five windows down each side. No stained glass, and a broken pane or two in the ordinary glass. Up front, the rudely fashioned pulpit sat on a plain wooden dais about six inches higher than the rest of the floor. An old upright piano sat against the front wall on the right side of the pulpit. Rough, handmade pews, constructed of one-by-threes spaced several inches apart, surrounded the dais and ran back the length of the church. They seated about a hundred people comfortably.

"Comfortably" refers to the amount of space, not the coziness of the pews. They were hard, unyielding benches, not well designed for the contour of the human anatomy. A few older folks brought pillows from home to employ as cushions. Others merely squirmed and readjusted themselves from time to time. I always imagined that the men who sat astride tractors most of the week were better prepared for the austerity of those benches than the rest of us.

The offerings in Poplar Grove Baptist Church were minuscule by most churches' standards. The intention each Sunday was to collect enough to pay the preacher his twenty-five dollar salary and have enough left over to help with the light bill. There was only a small heat bill. We had an old-fashioned pot-bellied stove in the middle of the building that was fed huge chunks of coal from a pile at the side of the building. If the weather was bad or there was an outbreak of flu, we didn't manage to collect thirty dollars, or even twenty-five. Some Sunday evenings my wife and I drove back to the university with a paper sack containing seventeen or eighteen dollars in pennies, nickels, dimes, and quarters. I don't remember that there was ever a dollar bill.

But what those poor farmers and their families lacked in monetary goods they made up for in hospitality and love. Almost every Sunday one of the elderly women would announce that she was preparing dinner for us and "some other folks too." There might be a dozen guests at the table and it might have taken two or three ladies an hour to get the food onto the table, but there was always plenty and it was accompanied by laughter and good companionship. In the fall, at hog-killing time, people often whispered to me, "There's a little something in your car," and it would be some ribs or a tenderloin. In the summers, the sacks would contain tomatoes, potatoes, beans, or ears of corn.

In the large metropolitan churches I pastored, it was different. The buildings were large and ornate. They had high-vaulted ceilings, great chandeliers, magnificent stained-glass windows, highly-polished chancel furniture, padded pews, silver communion ware, marble floors with carpeted walkways, and enormous pipe organs that cost more to maintain than the annual budgets of my smaller churches. Hundreds of people poured into the sanctuary each Sunday dressed in the latest fashions, the women with their hair done at expensive salons and smelling of high-priced perfume. They paid me well and the payments were never late or lacking. But there was never "a little something" slipped into our car, and only rarely did anybody say, "Let's go out to dinner together."

These were busy professional people, for the most part—doctors and attorneys and bankers and engineers; board chairmen and school board members; city planners and professors and librarians—the movers and shakers and sustainers of the community. They didn't have time for "getting together." They barely had time to come to church. Then they had to rush off to the country club for a quick lunch before eighteen holes of golf or a trip to the lake house or taking off on a plane for some distant city.

They *did* care about their churches' appearances. No squalid little frame buildings for them. No, indeed. They wanted big, glorious edifices that made a statement about who they were in the community and beyond. Everything freshly polished. No spots on the carpets. Huge furnaces and air conditioners that worked flawlessly to keep the sanctuary and classrooms at precisely the right temperatures all the time. Seamless parking lots and driveways without potholes. Attractive gardens with the trees and hedges all perfectly trimmed, and rose bushes healthy and productive, deeply mulched and carefully fertilized.

Those churches were wealthy—huge properties, big endowments, strong investments, large contributions, impressive budgets, respectable salaries, sizable donations to designated causes. Everything about them smelled of wealth, prestige, power, taste, and an infinite care about nonessentials.

Nonessentials, that is, as far as real church is concerned. As far as what Jesus was about, and the people he cared for. Jesus, the itinerant rabbi. Jesus, the mendicant Savior. Jesus, whose only property when he died was a robe and a pair of sandals. (By the way, did you ever wonder who got the sandals?)

I still recall the furor years ago when a minister at First Presbyterian Church of Chicago named John Frye fought for his board's permission to allow a group of young African Americans calling themselves the Blackstone Rangers to use the church's gym as a place to play and hang out. It was such a melee that it got into the papers. Frye and his followers won, but he didn't hang around long after that, probably for good reason.

The righteous guardians of that church's property didn't want a gang of hoodlums defiling their sacred space. What was worse, they didn't want them messing it up—smoking reefers, tracking in dirt, scratching the polished floors, breaking the furniture, putting graffiti on the walls, and generally desecrating the place for regular church members.

It was a symbolic fight, more important for what it said about most church members and their property than it said about Frye and Blackstone Rangers and the times. What's the old phrase, "Not in my backyard"? Exactly. The church is about love and reconciliation and taking care of the less fortunate, but please, somewhere else, on somebody else's turf, not on ours. It's more desirable to send our money to a missions board somewhere and let them spend it in Africa or South America providing medical aid to the sick and food for the poor than it is to start a clinic on our own property.

Most middle- and upper-class church members are very protective of their personal property rights, and this protectivism carries over to their church property as well. They didn't make it out of the deteriorating inner city into the pleasanter suburbs, where they could have beautiful lawns and shrubbery and decorative trees, only to have their property devalued by having the wrong kind of neighbors or the wrong kind of people using their facilities!

I don't have anything against beautiful churches. I love visiting grand cathedrals. I've spent hours in Chartres and Sacre Coeur and Notre Dame and St. Peter's and St. Patrick's and Canterbury and Westminster Abbey and Kaiser Wilhelm Memorial Kirche and dozens of other magnificent buildings. And I can almost accept the rationale somebody once gave me in Chichicastenango, in the mountains of Guatemala, when I expressed dismay at the beauty of the cathedral there in the midst of the abject poverty around it: "Yes, but isn't it wonderful for these poor people to have such a beautiful place for their prayers and worship! They have so little, and this is a kind of compensation."

I can almost accept it, but not quite. A part of me still rebels the way Luther did when he was crawling on his knees up the steps of the still-in-progress St. Peter's in Rome and asked, "Is this what Christ died for, to erect enormous monuments in his name? Is this what Paul spent a lifetime fighting for all over the face of the Roman Empire? Is this what three centuries of martyrs died for? These high towers, vaulted ceilings, marble floors, and golden candlesticks?"

Christianity is not really a monumental faith, or ought not to give that impression. It is a faith of the hustings, the barrio, the ghetto, a faith of prisons and factories and sweathouses, a faith of the marketplace and milling crowds. As long as there are still poor people on earth, people who drink from fetid pools and polluted streams, who die by the thousands because of typhoid and dysentery and AIDS, who try to coax a few beans or squash from barren, worn-out soil, who live in poverty and squalor and hopelessness, there ought not to be a beautiful, elegant, and expensive church building anywhere in the world.

And buildings are only the surface of the matter, because they are only the outward and visible sign of the personal greed and materialism so rampant among Christians, that choke off any witness we might give before we can even think about offering it, because we have done so little to combat poverty and sickness in the world.

A friend once gave me a large, handsomely produced book called *Material World: A Global Family Portrait*. It was a picture book about what the various peoples of the world possess. Most of the families in such lands as Ethiopia, India, Bhutan, Cuba, Haiti, and Albania have very little. The sum total of their possessions can be displayed in a tiny space, sometimes on a single blanket. Families in such countries as Russia, Italy, and Great Britain have more, and their possessions are shown cluttering their lawns. But in the U.S. it takes a doublewide driveway and the whole street outside for only part of the items from an average household of four persons. There's something wrong about this in a nation that often regards itself as the most Christian nation in the world. If we're so Christian, why do we have so much?

This kind of disparity is a constant theme in the Gospel of Luke, where Jesus tells the story of the Rich Fool, who plans to tear down his old barns and build greater ones to contain the enormous yield of his crops so he can say to his soul, "Soul, you have ample goods laid up for many years; relax, eat, drink, be merry!" But God says: "You fool! This very night your life is being demanded of you. And the things you have prepared, whose will they be?" (Luke 12:19–20)

Later, Jesus meets a wealthy ruler who wants to know what he must do to inherit eternal life. Jesus answers that the man already knows the commandments. He admits that he does, and has always kept them. "There is still one thing lacking," says Jesus. "Sell all that you own and distribute the money to the poor, and you will have treasure in heaven; then come, follow me." The man is disturbed about this, because he is extremely rich.

Jesus says a very hard thing: "It is easier for a camel to go through the eye of a needle than for someone who is rich to enter the kingdom of God" (Luke 18:18–25).

Luke then tells the story of Jesus's encounter with Zacchaeus, a tax collector in the city of Jericho. He doesn't tell us a lot, only that Jesus went to dine with him amidst a lot of tongue-wagging about his eating with a sinner. But obviously Jesus's gesture has a huge effect on Zacchaeus, who pledges to divest himself of half of everything he owns and give the money to the poor. Even more, he promises that if he has defrauded anyone, he will make restitution at the rate of 400 percent!

What is Jesus's response? He says that salvation has come to Zacchaeus's house, and he is a son of Abraham. This was the kind of behavior he wanted to see, and that Luke set at the center of his mission.

How many churches behave like Zacchaeus?

Once, when I was minister of the First Congregational Church of Los Angeles, I tried to plant a seed for such an action at a future time. It was Pentecost, and I was preaching on the story in Acts about the Jews who were gathered in Jerusalem when the Spirit of God came upon them in such amazing force that it overcame everything dividing them, even their various languages. I talked about what happens when the Spirit of God overrules our earthly ways of seeing and relating.

Suppose ten years from now, I said, those still here are gathered for a service like this. The years have taken their toll and not many of us are left. Because there are so few, the minister suggests that instead of his preaching, they do as the Quakers do, and sit quietly, waiting for enlightenment, and then share any insight they have been given.

After a few minutes of quiet time, a man stands to speak. God has put it in his heart, he says, that the people who own this magnificent building—for it was indeed magnificent!—should approach one of the many large Korean congregations meeting in theaters and store buildings and say to them, "God has given us this commodious church building and we have used it for many years. Now he wants you to have it, so we are turning it over to you. And perhaps, if the time comes when you no longer need such a building, you will surrender it to someone else."

I had not finished my sermon when the president of the Women's Association stood and walked out. By nightfall, powerful members of the board of deacons and the board of trustees were seeking my impeachment as their minister because I had proposed giving away their wonderful building!

My seed, unfortunately, did not germinate. I have been gone twenty years, and the congregation has in that time dwindled to an embarrassingly small number of constituents. The per-capita cost of maintaining such a property is scandalous. The security service alone costs more than $1,000 per member. Yet there is still no talk of ceding it to a Korean congregation or anyone else.

What would Jesus say?

Probably something apocalyptic, like the things he said about the temple in his own day, that it was only a pile of stones that would one day lie scattered like so many children's blocks.

(3) The Church's Lack of Courage

There is no adequate way of measuring comparative courage in human beings, but Jesus was surely one of the most courageous. He never flinched at speaking truth to power, whether he faced some quarrelsome scribe or stood before the Roman procurator. We are told by Luke that he "set his face toward Jerusalem" even though he knew the Holy City would be his undoing. And he appears to have confronted his death on the cross with unwavering equanimity and determination.

Ernest Hemingway, the novelist, had great respect for courage. He wrote about it in warriors, in bullfighters, and in ordinary persons facing hard situations. In *Death in the Afternoon*, he wrote admiringly of the toreros and toreadors who faced death unflinchingly every day in the bullring. And in a brief, little known play called *Today Is Friday*, in which he invented a conversation between two soldiers at a bar who had earlier presided over Jesus's death, he had them agree, "He was good in there today." It was the highest praise Hemingway, an avowed secularist and unbeliever, could pay. He placed Jesus in the company of the toreadors, who daily worked close to the razor-sharp horns of the bull without counting the consequences.

The early church drew its own conclusions about how Jesus and his disciples differed in this. He remained faithful to the end—a horrible, agonizing end—while they fled for their lives. Even the redoubtable Simon Peter, who had blusteringly whipped out his sword and taken off the ear of someone with the soldiers who accosted them in the garden, caved in and denied his Master to save himself.

There have been legends and stories of courageous believers through the ages, saints who endured persecution or death rather than perjure themselves before enemies of the faith—Joan of Arc perishing in the flames, Cranmer thrusting into the fire the hand that had signed a recantation, Anne Robinson going into banishment in New England, Albert Schweitzer burying himself in Africa for Christ's little ones, Martin Luther King Jr. dying by a shot from a cowardly assassin in Memphis, and dozens of heroic figures who endured death or imprisonment at the hands of modern atheists in charge of their countries.

I always marveled at the story my friend Sasha Makovkin, a potter in Mendocino, California, tells about his uncle in Russia, who during the revolution was called out into the town square before the church where he was a priest and offered his life in exchange for treading on the church's crosses and icons that the soldiers had spread on the cobblestones. He refused and was shot.

We admire such tales because of the paucity of heroes. Most Christians are more akin to the bishop who survived the tumultuous years of England's religious wars between the Catholics and Anglicans. Asked how he did it, he replied quite simply: "I smacked more of the willow than I did of the oak."

Most churches are virtual willow groves.

Mine in Los Angeles was.

It was in an area of town where there were many poor and homeless. Every morning when I arrived at the church there was a line of fifty or sixty people waiting for assistance of some kind. Many were ragged, dirty folks pushing grocery carts, pulling suitcases, or hauling around big plastic bags containing all their earthly possessions. One of their biggest problems was finding bathrooms they could use. McDonald's and other fast-food restaurants had posted guards to keep out anyone who wasn't a patron. The homeless had to resort to going in alleys and behind bushes in the park, but they often got busted by the police for doing so.

So I asked our trustees one night why we shouldn't rent a row of portaloos, as the British call them, and stand them sentinel-like in one of our parking lots as part of our ministry to the poor.

You'd have thought I had suggested bombing the *Los Angeles Times* or starting World War III! I hadn't imagined how many arguments could be summoned against such a charitable act. Think of the liability, the lawyers said, citing the school on our premises. What would happen if a homeless man molested a child or a teacher? The women of the church would be afraid to come to their weekday meetings. And the aesthetics of it were clearly unimaginable—fifteen or twenty bright blue portajohns (or red or whatever color they happened to be) arrayed against the majestic backdrop of our beautiful stone edifice!

I didn't get the portajohns for the poor, and the vote against them became one more vote for me to leave as the church's pastor. Somehow I sensed there was an unconscionable disconnect between the gospel I was trying to preach every Sunday and the church's lack of courage and commitment to do the right thing for Christ and the people who would have mattered most to him.

I couldn't help remembering Willie Creech. Willie was a short, stocky, coarse-haired man in little Poplar Grove Baptist Church back in Rockcastle County, Kentucky. Once a coal miner in West Virginia, he had carried a pistol on his hip during the bloody movement to unionize the mine workers. After his little daughter Faye was born, he wanted a safer place for her to grow up, so he moved his family to a small, hardscrabble farm in Kentucky. Willie had only been to the fourth grade, and still spoke with some of the archaic expressions he had learned as a boy, saying *hope* for "helped" and *stowed-ed* for "bestowed." But he was one of the finest men I ever knew.

Often, in business meetings of our little congregation, Willie took the hard or unpopular side of an issue. He would sit there erectly on the unforgiving board pew, his blue eyes shining as bright as a summer's sky, and say, as he pointed his finger toward heaven, "It's what *he* would want" or, "That's the way *he* would do it."

I wished for a few Willies on the board of trustees of that wealthy old church in Los Angeles. Even one or two would have made an enormous difference.

Now I look back across my lifetime and think how few times I ever knew the church to behave heroically. Almost always, the leading figures, the ones who affected the outcomes of all the votes, responded in cowardly fashion to the issues that came before them. They didn't ask what *he* would want, or, if they did, they never let on. Invariably, they took the easy or popular or sensible way, never the hard or dangerous way, never the adventurous way, never the way that might have led to a cross.

And that's why now, in my retirement years, I find an intolerable disjunction between Jesus and the church.

(4) The Church's Lack of Compassion

If there is one thing worse than the church's lack of courage when it faces the world around it, it's the church's dearth of compassion. To me, that is the most unforgivable sin of the church. There are always a few members of the church who do have a spirit of love and kindness; but the church as a whole often fails to display it. There is an almost unbelievable disconnect between the compassion of Jesus and that of the church.

Most ministers I know complain that there are cold and unfeeling people in their parishes, and some who are even hateful and malevolent. And somehow these people manage to cause untold damage to their churches' fellowship and destroy the churches' witness in their communities.

I can never forget the pain in the heart of a young female student at Claremont School of Theology who came to me with a sad story. She was an intern in a nearby church, and was aware that some of the members of the church wanted to get rid of the pastor they didn't like.

One Saturday night, she returned to the church to pick up a book she needed for the preparation of her Sunday school lesson. When she got there, she noticed there were lights in part of the building that weren't normally on at night. Approaching cautiously to look inside before entering, she was astounded at what she saw. Several of the pastor's enemies were emptying waste cans on the floor, writing slogans on the blackboards, and generally trashing the classrooms.

She knew these same people had complained to the board that the minister didn't police the custodial staff as he should. Now they were making it appear as if the minister's carelessness had resulted in intolerable messiness.

"I don't know if I can go on with my studies and become a minister," confessed the young woman. "I had no idea people in churches behaved like that. I'm not sure I could put up with that kind of behavior."

A member of a church in Tennessee told me about the meanness that surfaced in some board members when they learned that the pastor the church had called had a retarded daughter. Prior to moving to the community, the new pastor requested that the rooms of the parsonage be painted in differing colors so their daughter could more easily distinguish them.

Several members of the building committee refused, saying that they would never permit the new pastor to "deface" their property, as they didn't expect him to be their minister for very long anyway.

Harry R. Butman, a distinguished Congregationalist minister who lived to be a hundred, wrote a book in his last years called *Why Do Church People Fight?* One reason, he suggested, is that many of their favorite hymns encourage a truculent, warlike spirit. Every church hymnal, he said, contains "an astonishing number of hymns with military themes." Among the ones he cited were "The Son of God Goes Forth to War," "Onward, Christian Soldiers," "Stand Up, Stand Up for Jesus," and "Soldiers of Christ, Arise." Then he focused on one of everyone's favorite hymns, "The Battle Hymn of the Republic," in which, he reminded us, "the Lord can be seen in 'the watchfires of a hundred circling camps' with his 'terrible swift sword' in his hand and his 'trumpet that shall ne'er sound defeat'—a deity more like pagan Mars, the god of war, than the God of the Bible who made love the Great Commandment."[13]

There may be some truth in this observation. The British pastor-scholar H. H. Farmer once observed that there is something incredibly warlike in even the mildest person, so that he or she occasionally wants to take a whack at something, even if it is only the head of a dandelion.

---

13. Butman, *Why Do Church People Fight?*, 19–20.

But I fear it is much worse than this. I think it has to do with a streak of unconverted meanness and obstreperousness in some people, a dark side of their souls that has never been exposed to the love and compassion of the divine heart.

The Old Testament is filled with warlike imagery, and there are echoes of this destructive attitude in the Book of Revelation. But the Christ of the Gospels was never like this. He healed and fed people because he had compassion for them. He bade his disciples to love one another as he loved them, even to the point of sacrificing their lives. He prayed for his enemies even as his life ebbed away on the cross. And it is this picture, of a loving, forgiving, reconciling Christ, that informs—or ought to inform—the theology of the church, not the other picture, of people invariably fighting and quarreling and seeking the upper hand.

I always believed that the Reverend Jerry Falwell's frequently angry, judgmental, and injudicious remarks about liberals, abortionists, homosexuals, intellectuals, the ACLU, and anybody who disagreed with him were at least in part owing to his greater familiarity with the Old Testament than his dwelling in the spirit of the new covenant.

James J. H. Price, a fine biblical scholar at Lynchburg College, once delivered a paper to the Department of Religion at the University of Virginia on Falwell's use of the Bible, in which he observed that an inordinate amount of Falwell's preaching—90 percent is the figure I remember—was derived from Old Testament texts and not from the New Testament. Perhaps Falwell would not have been so outspokenly bellicose if he had been more steeped in the New Testament spirit of Christ.

It never ceases to amaze me that Christians who have read the Bible, listened to preaching, and meditated over the bread and wine of communion can be as vitriolic as some of them are, despising their ministers, reviling one another, striking out at the world, and generally behaving like total strangers to the gospel. It is as if their minds and hearts are completely compartmentalized, so that the gentler, kinder aspects of grace never actually penetrate into their inner beings at all.

I'm particularly appalled at how disturbed and overwrought ordinary church members can become in any discussion of homosexuality in today's society. A neighbor of ours, normally a very pleasant Christian woman, discovered that we had invited some gay friends from one of my former pastorates to attend an anniversary celebration.

"How can you possibly allow those people in your home?!" she demanded. "If a homosexual came to my door, I would slam it in his face!"

This woman attends church every Sunday, belongs to a Christian women's club, and enjoys going to two or three Bible study groups. She is proud of the fact that her children have grown up in a Christian home and have become stalwart figures in their respective churches as young adults. Yet it never seems to occur to her that there is anything about her frenzied intolerance that is incompatible with Christ's teachings about love and forgiveness.

Whole denominations, unfortunately, are being split apart today by this kind of rabid intolerance. Thousands of Christians rail against the appointment of homosexual priests, ministers, and bishops, insisting that it is "unscriptural" and "unchristian." Somehow it never dawns on them that they are being far more unscriptural by hating their brothers and sisters than their brothers and sisters are by loving persons of the same sex as themselves.

I can never forget something that happened on Thanksgiving Day at my church in Los Angeles. We had just completed a wonderful interfaith service in which the Jewish Torah scroll was carried in procession with the Christian flag. Baptists, Congregationalists, Disciples, United Methodists, Nazarenes, Roman Catholics, and Jews had worshiped together in what was called

"The Mayor's Thanksgiving Service" because Mayor Tom Bradley came each year and brought greetings to the congregation.

A few of us were standing in the church's lovely forecourt, basking in mild sunlight as we savored the afterglow of the service. Out of the corner of my eye, I saw a figure emerge from the trees beside the church and approach. It was an unkempt, disheveled man, probably in his forties, whose clothes were dirty and smeared with blood. He had plastic bags tied around his feet, which were otherwise bare. Apologizing for his appearance, he explained that he had been mugged the night before while sleeping in a nearby park. Some hoodlums had beat him up and stolen his wallet and his shoes.

"I have AIDS," he announced, "and my parents won't let me come home."

He said he was hungry and asked if we had any food.

We didn't, unfortunately, but I went into the church to get him some coffee. I filled the cup halfway with cream and sugar, so that he would get as much nourishment as possible. I also took time to telephone a hospice our church worked with and arranged for him to be admitted, knowing that he would receive a hot Thanksgiving meal and be cared for as long as necessary.

When I returned with the coffee, he was fondling a beautiful cloisonné necklace my wife was wearing. She told me later that he had admired it and asked if he could touch it.

Then, sensing my wife's compassion, he asked if she would give him a hug. He said he missed his mother's arms.

They hugged, and both of them wept.

"Would you mind if I gave you a kiss?" he asked.

Later, Anne said her first thought was, "Will I get AIDS?" At that time, not a great deal was known about the transmission of the disease. But she was so moved that she said "Of course," and moved closer for him to kiss her on the cheek.

Presently a taxi came and I bundled the man into it, paid the driver, gave him the address of the hospice, and told the man I would come to see him later. Our little group was now much quieter and soberer. Our previous exuberance in the festivity of the day had been affected by this sad encounter.

When Anne and I arrived home, the telephone was ringing. It was the vice president of the women's group at the church and she wanted to speak to Anne. I heard Anne stammer a bit and then saw the tears sliding down her face.

The woman had attacked her viciously, saying that she and some other women had seen our meeting with the stranger in the forecourt and were outraged that their minister and minister's wife would have anything to do with such a shabby looking man.

"You have brought shame on your husband and on our church!" she declared in an angry voice.

It was then, I think, that I began seriously to think about leaving that church. How could anyone, I wondered, attend church regularly, listen to sermons about Christ and the gospel, and remain so utterly devoid of Christian love and compassion? And she was a leading member of the congregation.

An Actual Disjunction

It is unreasonable, I know, to judge an entire congregation on the performance of a single individual or even of several individuals. But sometimes we are driven over the edge of reason and become unreasonable.

I know that Christ has affected the hearts of millions of people through the ages, and that the churches of the world have produced hundreds of millions of saints. But there are times when I can't help thinking that the church in general has simply failed to reproduce the spirit of Christ in our time.

There is too vast a disjunction, after twenty centuries of struggle, between the Jesus of the Gospels—a man generous toward sinners, devoid of materialism, courageous, and filled with unbounded love and compassion—and the average church in our time. It is almost as if Jesus had nothing to do with the church, as if he hadn't walked the earth, as if he had taught nothing, as if he had not died a hideous death on the cross, as if he had not been raised from the dead to breathe as the heart and soul of a compassionate church.

Maybe our preaching and teaching are at fault, so that we haven't been able to convert people to the real Jesus, the Jesus whose very manner convinced some people that he was actually God, the Jesus whose name has been said to charm the stars from the skies and the guile from villains' hearts, the Jesus whose life and teachings, says Pelikan, "represented an answer (or, more often, *the* answer) to the most fundamental questions of human existence and human destiny."[14]

If the preaching and teaching haven't been that bad, perhaps there is something inherently wrong about human nature and it simply can't aspire to being more than it is.

Whatever it is, the disjunction is there, and I sense it more and more as I grow older, so that sometimes I awaken in a sweat and don't know what is the matter until I think for a moment and realize it is the disconnect itself, the disparity between what we know and what we do, that is troubling me. It is a problem I don't know how to fix, and it isn't enough for me to say, "That isn't my problem, it's God's; my business is to do the best I can and tend my own little garden," because my heart aches for something better, for the kingdom of God that Jesus has shown us but nobody seems to care about.

I'm overstating. Some people do care. But not many. Not enough. Certainly not a majority of church members.

14. Pelikan, *Jesus through the Centuries*, 2.

Toward the end of his long peroration in *Stealing Jesus* about how the Church of Love, Jesus's church, has become the Church of Law, Bruce Bawer tells about attending the trial of Episcopal Bishop Walter Righter, who was charged with violating church rules by ordaining a sexually active homosexual. Preparing for the trial, he placed telephone calls to a couple of the "presenters," bishops who were bringing the charges.

Bawer could hardly believe the enormity of their rancor, "their fierce determination to cling to manifest untruths about the nature of sexual orientation." That, together with "their enthusiasm for law, dogma, and institutional order," made it clear that they swore "allegiance to the Church of Law."

The morning of the hearing, Bawer shared a cab with one of the witnesses, a professor of theology who had written an essay declaring that homosexuality was a sign of the Fall of Man. Bawer found him too biased even to have a conversation with him.

At the cathedral, he took a seat in the press section of the large hall. He was sitting behind two men, one in a clerical collar and the other holding a large briefcase. The briefcase turned out to be full of propaganda against the accused bishop, which the man happily shoved at reporters around him.

Across the aisle sat a couple of presenters, surrounded by their supporters. Bawer studied their faces, trying to see something in them that would help him to understand their fervor for their cause.

Bawer, a homosexual himself, felt overwhelmed and yet strangely exhilarated by the situation. Almost everyone around him was fiercely opposed to homosexuals. At the end of the day, when the head of the court asked everyone to stand for prayer, he stood, bowed his head, and prayed in the midst of people he knew considered his life, his very identity, an abomination. And he prayed for *them*.

It was then, he wrote, "as I stood there praying, that I realized why I felt so joyful: It was because I knew that what these people thought about me ultimately didn't matter. What they did, ultimately didn't matter. I knew, not only in an abstract intellectual sense, but with all my heart and soul and strength, that however hard they tried, they *could not separate me from the love of God.*"[15]

He realized, in the end, that none of these people, who were his enemies as fully as they were Bishop Righter's enemies, could really steal Jesus from him, or could diminish the gift of love and inclusion Jesus had given him. He still clung to the essence of faith.

The others, unfortunately, didn't. Preening themselves on their righteousness, their knowledge of church law, and the popularity of their cause, they had abandoned Jesus and the church originally fashioned by men and women who had known Jesus.

They had given up the Church of Love, as Bawer called it, for the Church of Law.

15. Bawer, *Stealing Jesus*, 313.

5

The Absence of Spirituality in the Church

What was needed to uphold the old spirituality and
to educate its followers is quite different from what we
need now to guide us on a spiritual path.

—ELIZABETH LESSER, *THE NEW AMERICAN SPIRITUALITY*[1]

[There is] a new mood in Christendom, a more
conscious, general recognition that though for
Christians God is defined by Jesus, he is not confined to Jesus.

—HUSTON SMITH, *THE SOUL OF CHRISTIANITY*[2]

A religious person could surely have no higher goal than to become a truly spiritual being, one who lives daily in the presence of God with such a sense of awareness that the entire world becomes richer, sweeter, and more agonizingly beautiful. Our one tantalizing statement about Jesus between his dedication at the temple and his baptism and the commencement of his ministry says that he "grew in wisdom and stature, and in favor

1. Lesser, *The New American Spirituality*, 52.
2. Smith, *The Soul of Christianity*, 16.

with God and man" (Luke 2:52). It isn't much, but it does suggest a developing sense of awareness of the kind that ought to belong to an intermediary between heaven and earth.

Jesus frequently quoted the Psalms, indicating that he had stored them in his heart while a young man, and often recommended to the disciples that they be daily seekers of God as he was. He was who he was as a teacher and worker of miracles because he was a man of prayer and devotion. They were obviously his source of power.

When his disciples failed to cast out a demon, he told them, "This kind can come out only through prayer" (Mark 9:29). We often forget what a man of prayer he was. We remember him falsely as some kind of superhero who was able to perform wonders in and of himself, when in fact he was a deeply spiritual person whose connection with God was the secret of his whole life.

It is ironic that the church in our time should be so little committed to prayer and spirituality as a way of life. Part of the church is big on evangelism, and part is big on social action. And there is a lot of talk about prayer, and handbooks on how to pray. But there are few congregations where spirituality is faithfully emphasized, so that they have numerous prayer groups filled with genuinely spiritual people.

One reason may be that prayer has been cast in such a utilitarian light in a country whose predilection is for pragmatism. The best-selling book on prayer in several decades was Bruce Wilkinson's *The Prayer of Jabez,* a small volume embraced as a shortcut to success instead of as a treatment of transformative spirituality. The gurus of religion on television have all emphasized the practicality of prayer. They teach that God wants to give us everything we desire—better jobs, bigger houses, newer cars, our children's education, more successful marriages—implying that prayer is a simple mechanical arrangement whereby God gives us what we want if we only ask for it in the right way.[3] So most Christians today have tried prayer the way they have tried various diets and exercise plans, only to give it up in frustration when they don't see the results they seek in a relatively short time.

Few modern Christians ever undertake the life of prayer in order to become spiritual persons, seeking to be molded into godliness the way the young protagonist of Nathaniel Hawthorne's story, "The Great Stone Face," eventually began to resemble the figure whose face he had always studied on the side of the mountain. This kind of devotionalism is not recommended by many ministers because, in fact, they themselves have never become very adept at it and sensed as a result that their own lives and desires were being altered by it.

The Roman Catholic Church and the Orthodox Church have always had a fall-back position in their monasteries, where monks and nuns spend so much time in prayer and devotion that it becomes second nature to them. Someone once argued—I forget who but still agree—that these centers of spirituality may be the very salvation of the world. Yet even in these places there is a certain spottiness about the real spiritual life. Some seekers attain it and others don't.

I have long enjoyed W. Paul Jones's personal story in *The Province Beyond the River: The Diary of a Protestant at a Trappist Monastery.* When I knew Jones a few years ago, he was a professor of theology at the St. Paul School of Theology in Kansas City,

---

3. Michael Spencer says: "The largest church in the United States is pastored by a motivational speaker who tells his audiences how to improve their lives with a positive attitude and relentless efforts to be nice. His best-selling book tells readers how to have their best life now, with 'the best' presented in unashamedly consumer-friendly, all-American terms. From getting a new house to finding a great parking space to simply being the one who always gets the goodies, this pastor leads millions of people every week to believe that Christianity is about you getting everything you want the way you like it so that you you you you . . ." (Spencer, *Mere Churchianity*, 29).

a United Methodist seminary. His book, cast in the form of an actual diary, is the narrative of his three-month sabbatical in a Trappist monastery high in the Rocky Mountains.

On the very first page, Jones admits: "I have never experienced God, not really. I am embarrassed by piety; I am ill at ease with those who thrive on God talk; I have no awareness of what one might mean by the 'presence of God.'"[4]

This is a weighty admission for a man who was a professor of theology. What does it say about what he taught his students for the years before he went to the monastery? Are there many such professors in seminaries? I have sometimes wondered, during my own years of teaching, about the spirituality of some of my colleagues. I recall one extremely well known professor of Old Testament who admitted to me when we were on a trip together that he had not really believed in God since he finished graduate school.

Jones's admission raises a very serious question, namely, is it possible that Christianity is *riddled* with unbelief because many of its greatest proponents have never actually experienced the presence of God, as Jones said he hadn't?

Jones did experience the presence of God that summer in the monastery. It happened to him one afternoon in the refectory, of all places. He had volunteered to help a lay brother who was charged with preparing food that day. He calls him "Bro. C." Bro. C, he said, was "a gracious, kindly, simple person with a finely honed sense of humor," but tended to deprecate himself because he didn't have as much learning and experience as the priests. He assumed Jones was a priest. Jones told him who he really was, and that he was there because, in spite of his position and years of training, he lacked what Bro. C had, an inner knowledge of God.

At this, Bro. C opened up to him in a new way.

There in that mundane setting, under the tutelage of a lay brother, "somewhere between the cauliflower and the squash,"

4. Jones, *The Province Beyond the River*, 3.

Jones discovered what he had been seeking. Bro. C taught him how to pray, and how to lose himself in the words he was praying.

Later that afternoon, Jones lost himself head-over-heels in two verses of scripture, "God is my possession forever" and "I will thank the Lord with all my heart."

In the evening, as he prepared for bed, he noticed that the mountain was emerging from a mist that had covered it, and, as he closed his drapes, "it was as if God were having fun. Like a painter in final delight, he put a dab of cloud at the very peak."[5]

The rest of the professor's summer was a celebration. He had experienced God. His faith had finally become real.

This is why Annie Dillard said in *Teaching a Stone to Talk* that people ought to wear crash helmets and strap themselves into the pews when they come to worship, because when we are dealing with God we are always facing the dangerous possibility that we shall be totally changed. All our old values can be transposed and we can become new creatures in Christ. We can, like Jones, lose all self-control.

Isn't this what is missing in so many churches and Christian gatherings? The people in them are still in control of their own lives and destinies. One hundred percent in control. And they don't really want to surrender that control. Not ultimately, or even to a significant degree. They're like the old-time photographs of maiden ladies in modest swimsuits posing at the edge of the water, perhaps daintily dipping a toe into the foam but hardly eager to plunge into the waves.

Despite years of education and a natural inclination toward being reserved and orderly, I greatly respect Pentecostal and Holiness groups that do surrender control when they worship. When I was a boy growing up in a town in Kentucky, I sometimes went down to the courthouse on Saturday evenings to watch the Holy Roller services. A preacher would be raising and lowering his

5. Ibid., 58.

voice, moaning and whining, waving his arms and stamping his feet, and sometimes throwing his head back so violently that I expected it to break his neck. All over the room, people would groan, speak in tongues, and pray aloud for the Spirit of God to overpower them. Eyes closed, faces contorted, they dipped and swayed, dancing in place, their arms tracing broken patterns in the air. Here and there, a few worshipers would have collapsed onto the benches or the floor, writhing in what to my young eyes appeared to be a fit, and moaning as if they were having orgasms.

Even then, I had a certain respect for such behavior, because I knew, in a society where they were mostly poor slaves of an economy that had forgotten them, they were escaping for a few minutes or even an hour or two into some wild, disorderly place of the soul where they were free and untrammeled. I don't know what the long term effects on them were. Probably afterward they returned to their normal existences as dishwashers and house maids and auto mechanics as soberly and prosaically as if they had been serious drinkers coming off a binge. But it is hard to believe they did not have some sense of residue from their time of abandonment, some feeling of having been with God in the flower-strewn meadows of the soul.

My friend Dennis Covington's book *Salvation on Sand Mountain* "knows" about this kind of thing. Dennis now teaches writing at North Texas State University, but before that he taught at the University of Alabama in Birmingham. While there, he served as a stringer for the *New York Times* in the southeastern U.S. He was sent, in that capacity, to cover the trial of a snake-handling minister in the Sand Mountain area of northern Alabama. The minister was being sued by his wife for endangerment because he forced her, purportedly testing her faith, to thrust her hand into a box of rattlesnakes.

Covington was so taken by the obvious sincerity and belief of the snake-handling cult that during the time of the trial and for weeks afterwards he visited the members in their homes and attended their services. He usually remained at the rear of the church as a measure of protection in case a snake got loose. But one evening he became so caught up in the rhythm of the castanets and clapping that he made his way to the front, reached into a cage of snakes, lifted out a big specimen, and waved it around his head before replacing it. Afterwards, he said, he sat in his car in the dark and trembled for half an hour before switching on the engine and returning to Birmingham.

It happened to him on a second occasion, and again he shook afterward as he reflected on what he had done. From then on he would not let himself attend another service, for fear that he would be caught up in the Spirit again and would be bitten.

Covington was a deacon in Southside Baptist Church in Birmingham, and so was his novelist wife Vicki. He had attended numerous revival meetings in which he had felt highly stimulated, but never like this. Snake-handling, he said, had changed him forever. He would never forget it and would never be the same man again.

Both these groups, the Holy Rollers of my youth and Covington's snake-handlers, were onto something more dramatic than I am seeking, but I think they offer a clue to the way real spirituality works. It works for people who commit themselves as fully as possible to the game and don't hold anything back in reserve— people who aren't into what Diarmuid O'Murchu calls "insipid religiosity."[6]

For me personally, true religion works better in quietness and solitude than in arenas of noisy demonstration. It works when I silently leap off the cliff of the known into the seas of God's love and grace—the unknown—without worrying about how I shall get back onto the ledge. It is more akin to what happened to Paul Jones "between the cauliflower and the squash," when he

6. O'Murchu, *Catching Up with Jesus*, 37–38.

discovered the divine presence and found rest in the words of the Bible and the images of his heart.

It is also more like the enlightenment that accompanies Zazen when Buddhist monks toy with a koan, one of those insoluble little enigmas assigned by a roshi, and are amazingly smitten by an insight that transcends the puzzle itself, or when other monks arrive at the same startling revelation by staring into a candle's wavering light or counting the breaths they take. All at once, say these monks, their vision of the world is changed. It is brighter, more alive, more vibrant than they ever knew it to be. The world hasn't changed, of course; they have. Their perceptions are inexplicably sharpened, so that now they view everything in vivid color instead of the pale, washed-out shades they saw before.

Buddhists like to talk about "awareness," which to them means being present to everything around them without needing to direct or control it. It is in one sense passive, but in another sense very interactive, because in this heightened state of sensibility, the mind becomes engaged in everything and is part of it. The Christian who learns to pray in a warm, receptive way, listening instead of talking, feels a similar oneness with everything, as if he or she were coextensive with the whole created order.

Speaking of listening reminds me of what Mother Teresa said when a reporter asked her what she said to God when she prayed.

"Oh, I don't say anything," the little woman replied. "I just listen."

"Ah," said the reporter, "and what does God say to you when you listen?"

"Nothing," she said. "He listens too."

There is a wonderful insight in that little story. Mother Teresa became directly connected with God when she prayed. She didn't have to say or hear anything for it to be a successful prayer. The connection was everything. It recharged her life with energy and awareness. It was the primary secret of her extraordinarily vital existence.

Unfortunately, I cannot point to a single church where I know there is any real training for this kind of spirituality. We Americans are so practical. We are taught to pray for specific things, to make lists and pray through them as if we were ordering groceries. Some teachers even recommend keeping lists of what we have prayed for and ticking off the answers as we see them appear in response to our prayers. There is rarely any suggestion in such teaching that answers don't really matter to the person who is seeking the divine presence and not specific blessings at all.

They don't, of course. When we abandon ourselves to the love of God, we experience an abundance of spirit that countermands all our hopes and desires.

In his classic study *Man against Himself,* psychologist Karl Menninger told the story of Father Doyle, a Roman Catholic chaplain in World War I, whose diary he had read. Father Doyle spent his days in combat, working with men in the trenches of what has often been described as "the bloodiest war in history." At night, he returned to his bunker, where he eagerly sought communion with God. Often, wrote Father Doyle, he felt so overwhelmed by ecstasy as he prayed that he was ashamed of being only one human heart experiencing and celebrating the love of God. He felt inundated, swept about, completely at the mercy of his heavenly Father.

I am sure Father Doyle did not go to God with a list of the things he must remember to pray for. Not that he did not pray for the soldiers who had died that day, or their families, or the other men who had been wounded in battle. But falling into the arms of God, for him, was tantamount to plunging into a bottomless sea of adoration where the soul could only flounder because it lost all perspective on earthly things.

Over the years, I have written several books of prayers,[7] and, in a modest way, I am understandably proud of some of them, and happy to know that other ministers use them as models for their own prayers and meditations on Sunday morning. They are often specific in the requests they make to God—for grace and peace for the worshipers, for renewal and strength for the sick or bereaved, for traveling mercies for visitors and protection for the young.

But I know these prayers are nothing in the total arena of prayer—*less* than nothing—because they are only beginning or (at best) elementary prayers, they are not the stuff of prayer like Father Doyle's or the prayers of any mystic who knows what it is to bask in the ineffable presence of the divine being.

The kind of praying we do in church or teach our students to do in youth groups or Sunday school classes is only kindergarten or grade-school prayer. It almost never reaches into high school, and, I would venture, definitely never achieves the level of college or graduate school. It is only an amateurish, slapdash kind of praying that has little to do with the development of real saints who will bring holiness and healing to a world desperately in need of God.

I have been interested in reading about the evangelist Billy Graham as he sat by his wife's bedside while she was dying and as he rocked on the front porch of his cabin near Montreat, North Carolina, looking out at the mist and the mountains. For years, when he was younger and was traveling the world as a preacher, Graham's prayers were for his revival campaigns, for the workers who prepared them, for the people he believed needed to be saved, for himself and the singers and others who were most responsible for the success of his meetings.

7. *Lost in Wonder, Love, and Praise; Enter Every Trembling Heart,* and *God's People at Prayer.*

But when he was old and infirm and no longer able to go out on campaigns, as his wife was dying and he himself was feeling the debilitations of age, he spent more time just being with God. He sat with his wife and he sat with God. It was a completely different kind of prayer—a prayer in which he rested in God and surrendered everything to God's will. There was no more anxiety to do well or to make a difference in the world. Now it was time to turn everything over to God, to relax, merely to be there with God.

How different our lives would be if we only learned to do this earlier instead of later in our lives. If we could only learn to leap off the cliff, to rest in the holy, to abandon our pretenses, anxieties, and ambitions in order merely to wait before God. If we could only be like the old Basque sheepherder who came into his hut at night, exhausted from a long day's work, and sighed, "*Seigneur, voilà Jean*"—"Lord, here is John."

A Lackluster Performance

The question persists: How is it that we have the most advanced sociological understanding of congregations in the history of the world, the largest, most comfortable buildings to meet in, the biggest libraries of books and music, and the most sophisticated aids ever devised, including CDs and DVDs and overhead projectors and all the rest, and we can go on offering such a thin and superficial understanding of prayer to our people? Thousands in worship. Outstanding choirs and vast, impressive organs. TV, Web, and radio broadcasts that carry our services for thousands of miles. And we do a poorer job of teaching people how to pray and become spiritual beings who live daily and hourly in the Spirit of God than the church of any era in history.

How do we explain it?

Just think, we have all these people in worship—an attorney going into an important litigation trial tomorrow under enormous pressure to perform; a student taking her SATs and facing the fact that her whole future may ride on the outcome; a woman scheduled for her first round of chemo after surgery didn't get all the bad cells of her breast cancer; a young soldier going back to Afghanistan for his second tour of duty; a young couple taking bankruptcy and surrendering their home; a couple about to adopt their first child; a gay man who has just opted to tell his parents about his sexual orientation; a surgeon starting a delicate brain operation at 6 a.m.; a young woman who recently discovered she has MS; a teenager whose biology teacher has been touching her inappropriately; and hundreds of others with similar cares and concerns.

They need to know how to pray and become spiritual persons. Why are we giving them stones instead of bread? Is it because the leaders in our churches and seminaries don't really know how themselves, and are only playing at being church and teaching people about God? Is it any wonder, given all this, that most of us outgrow the church after a few years and have to begin finding our own way on spiritual pilgrimages?

I have always loved the church. I want to go to church now. But when I do I almost always feel as if I have stepped back into play school and that nobody is making a serious effort to offer me anything that will help me to move on into the no-man's land of my later years. Nobody is tempting me to new and thrilling understandings of my journey. Nobody even seems to care that I am on a journey. It is all business as usual. Sunday after Sunday, always the same. We never climb to a higher level. We never really go anywhere. It is all very depressing.

In Dr. Maurice Rawlings's book *Beyond Death's Door*, he describes the near-death experience of one of his patients who remembered visiting heaven. When he was admitted through the pearly gates, he found everyone dressed in glowing white robes. His mother and father were there to greet him. His mother, who had been an amputee in her previous life, had her leg restored in her new existence. As they walked around, he noticed that one building was larger than all the others. It seemed to be as big as a football stadium, and one end was open, so that an incredibly bright light was emanating from it. "What is that?" he asked his parents.

"In there," they replied, "is God."[8]

I attempt to imagine there being a similar halo of light over churches where there is real spirituality at work. I can discern it over one or two, perhaps—unusual churches where the people are especially loving and sweet-spirited, so that they emanate a sense of divine presence to everyone passing by or stopping to visit. But not over many.

It is a pity. It ought to be over all the churches.

But then, that's our situation. Very few churches even understand or want to understand true spirituality.

Merging with Others

One final note: When we are being spiritual, we are moving closer and closer to spiritual persons in other religions, to what Teilhard de Chardin once called "the omega point" at which everything converges.[9] If we are merely religious, there are walls and hedges all around us that demarcate our territory from theirs. But if we transcend religion and become spiritual, then the walls and hedges disappear and increasingly we feel our commonality with others.

8. Rawlings, *Beyond Death's Door*, 99.

9. Cf. Elizabeth Lesser, *The New American Spirituality*, 23: "Widely different human cultures around the Earth are now converging toward an *omega point*," wrote Pierre Teilhard. "That seems to me the only possible conversion of the world, and the only form in which a religion of the future can be conceived."

I believe that was what was happening to Thomas Merton at the end of his life. Merton had always had a deeply spiritual inclination, ever since he was a student. He talked about this in *Seven Storey Mountain*, the biography of his earlier years. But his years of prayer and solitude at Gethsemani Abbey in Kentucky must have refined this inclination more and more, until he sought its natural issue, a relationship with like-minded people in other religions.

It was this that took him to Bangkok, where he died in a freakish accident. He had traveled there to explore the kinship of his faith with that of Zen Buddhists. If he had lived I expect we would have had a very rich book from him about Zen insights that Christians could appropriate for their own lives of prayer and meditation.

To me, this is part of what it means to outgrow church. It means feeling the kinship Merton was feeling and embracing people of other faiths in order to be more at home in our own faith. Unfortunately, there are not many churches where such kinship is even mentioned, much less explored or cultivated with any enthusiasm. A few Unitarian-Universalist churches, perhaps, and an even smaller number of UCC churches. We are still prisoners of our old Me-Tarzan-You-Jane mentality, the one where we felt safely preeminent and right about our own beliefs and sent missionaries to people in other countries in an effort to "enlighten" them.

Kinship. It is what three women in New York discovered after the terrorist attack on the World Trade Center in 2001. Feeling alone and confused, not knowing what to say to her daughter, who found herself the object of many questions from Jewish and Christian schoolmates, a Palestinian Muslim woman named Ranya decided that she needed to explore the meaning of faith and community with people who were not of her own background. She got in touch with two women, an ex-Catholic named Suzanne and a Jew named Priscilla. Her proposal to them was that the three of them meet regularly for coffee and discussions and that they collaborate on a book for children about the common origins of their three faiths. The result was a book about their dialogue called *The Faith Club*.[10]

Over the next few months, the women talked openly and sometimes critically about their religions. For example, Suzanne said she had left the Catholic Church and become an Episcopalian because she and her husband were turned off by the priests' "uninspiring sermons," the church's position on social issues, and its overall rigidity. Priscilla said she wasn't even sure there was a God. Then one day, in a moment of rare intimacy when they were discussing death, she blurted out, "I wish I believed in God." Nobody in her family, she said, had ever talked about God. In twenty years of marriage, she and her husband had had only one two-minute conversation about God. Eventually, through such a growing sense of togetherness, Suzanne and Priscilla began reading the Quran and trying to see the world through Ranya's eyes. The three of them found themselves discussing God and the meaning of life and death on a regular basis. Each contributed helpful thoughts and ideas from her own background. They shared their personal and family problems, and learned that they were growing in their ability to handle these problems because of their collaborative experience.

Eventually each woman developed a profound respect for the faiths of the others. Suzanne vocalized her disagreement with fellow Christians who thought their religion was the only path to God. "In their hands," she said, "Jesus seemed to become a polarizing force rather than a unifying one."[11]

"I wasn't sure Jesus' savior role was that important to my conception of God," she wrote, thinking about the matter. "I related to

10. Idiby, Oliver, and Warner, *The Faith Club*.
11. Ibid., 199.

Jesus as my brother and my teacher. He helped me understand the qualities of God. He was the conduit to something much greater. I realized I never addressed Jesus when I prayed. I directed my prayers straight to God, my creator and my judge. Jesus felt too human next to the vast power I imagined when I thought of God."[12]

The three women began attending one another's religious services together. Ranya, who had started the meetings, confessed that she had become "more of a believer" because of what she learned about the other women's faiths. She realized that what really attracted her to religion in the first place was the sense of community with which it endowed her life, and being with the other two women had strengthened that sense more than anything she had ever experienced. Suzanne agreed. She had embraced other religions, she said, and had become a universalist. There were still many things to figure out, but one big area of agreement had taken over her life: "that we should love God with all our heart, soul, mind, and strength and love our neighbor as ourselves."[13]

Most Christian pastors fear being politically incorrect with their congregations by suggesting there could be anything worthwhile in other religions. They are paid their salaries to uphold the prejudices and orthodoxies of their churches. So they grind out their days, some of them knowing better and feeling slightly guilty, in the same sing-song, treadmill way we have of rocking along in the same old rut, and live safely instead of adventurously.

That's a big mistake, in individuals or in churches. It is *adventure* that keeps us alive!

12. Ibid.
13. Ibid., 277.

6

Mr. Darwin Isn't the Enemy

Christian fundamentalists reject the discoveries of
of biology and physics about the origins of life and insist
that the Book of Genesis is scientifically sound in every detail.

—KAREN ARMSTRONG, *THE BATTLE FOR GOD*[1]

When I left the full-time practice of science and
turned my collar around to become a clergyman, my life
changed in all sorts of ways. One important thing did not
change, however, for, in both my careers, I have been
concerned with the search for truth.

—JOHN POLKINGHORNE, *QUARKS, CHAOS, AND CHRISTIANITY*[2]

The last time I attempted to worship in our local Presbyterian
church, I was defeated by a minister who employed his
sermon time—all twenty minutes of it—in a ludicrously heroic
attempt to prove that Charles Darwin couldn't have been right because natural selection was simply not God's way. All the efforts of
geologists and cosmologists to prove that the world is older than
Bishop Ussher's chronology allows are simply misleading and er-

1. Armstrong, *The Battle for God*, xi.
2. Polkinghorne, *Quarks, Chaos, and Christianity*, 115.

roneous, he said, because they are bent on destroying our faith in the book of Genesis. Even the skeletal remains of prehistoric monsters are a lie concocted to divert us from the fact that God created the world in six days and there is no reference to them in scripture.

I could only imagine what an intimidating sermon series this stalwart pastor—who was, incidentally, a former Baltimore policeman for whom ministry was a second career—could wheel out against the ungodly proponents of relativity, DNA, the Big Bang theory, cosmic microwave background radiation, and other hot button topics of recent science, most of which are far more threatening to the old creeds and theologies than poor old Darwin ever thought of being.

His diatribe against the discoveries of the last two centuries reminded me of how reluctant religious conservatives are to have any truck at all with modern science and how confused the rest of us are because we have had so little instruction in the church about how to square the classic doctrines of our faith with the scientific truths we feel bound to accept.

Chet Raymo, a former teacher and science columnist for *The Boston Globe*, says in *When God Is Gone Everything Is Holy* that religion and science are the two greatest forces in the world and the tension between them remains "palpable and real." In his own religion of Catholicism, the battle with the *content* of science is largely over; but theological orthodoxy's battle with the *spirit* of the scientific approach has been generally swept under the rug. "*Theologically,*" he says, "it's as if the Scientific Revolution never happened. We teach twenty-first-century science in the classroom, and in the chapel we recite a Creed based on neolithic cosmologies."[3]

As Hamlet would say, "there's the rub." We have not, in the church, addressed the problem of truly reconciling old theologies

3. Raymo, *When God Is Gone Everything Is Holy*, 107–8.

and new science. Consequently, most of us attempt to live in both worlds by avoiding the more obvious contradictions. We recite "I believe in God . . . Maker of heaven and earth" on Sunday and believe in the Big Bang theory and paleolithic monsters the rest of the week. We pray to God to save us from dreaded diseases, yet rush to the doctor the minute we develop a symptom. Many of us resisted funding for stem-cell research, accepting that it was somehow anti-religious, but clamor for it if we have a spinal injury or some other problem in which it has proved efficacious.

Because we have not as a society openly and aggressively explored the relationship between belief and empiricism, we are left to fend for ourselves individually when faced with life's most perplexing questions. For example, my wife and I recently sat with a dear friend as she lay dying. My wife said afterward that she felt as if she actually intruded into our friend's death, and it left her with great uneasiness about what she believed. Did she believe our friend's soul was going straight to God? Or did she believe, like most neurobiologists, that when her brain activity ceased she was simply gone, and that was that? How was she—my wife—to reconcile her religious faith and her scientific understanding?

It is possible that we shall never be able to achieve total reconciliation of the two, but it is obvious that we must do a far better job than we have been doing up to now. And the first order of business is to face the fact that our faith derives from one cultural era and our scientific knowledge from another, and to ask how we can possibly synthesize them in a way that does not do unjustifiable harm to either. Theologians and pastors have for too long accused scientists of being anti-religious when in actuality they have not been that at all, but have remained silent about faith, waiting for the theologians to do their proper work of helping religious people to modulate between an age of wonder and an age of investigation.

The modern Christian has many questions about faith that no one has even attempted to answer with any scientific credibility: What is the nature of the soul? What happens when we die? Where is heaven? Will we recognize our loved ones in the beyond? Does God really answer prayer or is it, as Freud said, only "wishful thinking"? Is there actually something called "the will of God" or is everything only happenstance?

Why can't theologians stop doing evasive fandangos around creedal statements and come to terms with the fact that we live in a universe far more exciting than the early church realized? Must discoveries of new galaxies in space and new complexities in the human genetic system always be greeted with fear and distrust because they weren't spelled out in biblical literature penned centuries ago? I like the quotation from Carl Sagan's *Pale Blue Dot* cited by Richard Dawkins in *The God Delusion*:

> How is it that hardly any major religion has looked at science and concluded, "This is better than we thought! The Universe is much bigger than our prophets said, grander, more subtle, more elegant"? Instead they say, "No, no, no! My god is a little god, and I want him to stay that way." A religion, old or new, that stressed the magnificence of the Universe as revealed by modern science might be able to draw forth reserves of reverence and awe hardly tapped by the conventional faiths.[4]

I totally agree. Sagan was right, and Dawkins right in quoting him. The church—one of the "conventional faiths"—has been too fearful about admitting that the playing field is much larger and other than the area staked out by ancient prophets and priests, because it knows that the admission would instantly threaten a lot of outmoded assumptions about God and life and its own rituals and protocols. There are some things in our religion we have not outgrown and never shall—expressions of awe and wonder before the marvels of creation, appraisals of self and society before the

4. Dawkins, *The God Delusion*, 12.

limitlessness of God, inculcations to love and joy and celebration. These are ageless responses, and entirely worthy. But to declare our minds and systems closed against new readings of the nature of self, God, and universe is sheer foolishness. Even worse, it is a form of blasphemy!

I like the analogy Chet Raymo uses in *Honey from Stone*, that human knowledge is like a finite island in the midst of an infinite sea of mystery. Increasing our knowledge, so that the circumference of the island is enlarged, does not diminish the mystery; it only lengthens the shoreline along which we can understand or relate to it. What we know of biology and chemistry and geology and psychology and all the other spheres of knowledge does not make us atheists or even agnostics, it merely enables us to penetrate the Cloud of Unknowing in new and exciting ways.

What did the Apostle Paul say? "When I was a child, I thought as a child" (1 Cor 13:11). Of course! That is the nub of the matter. In comparison with what human beings will know a century or two from now, we are still benighted; but compared to what the ancient prophets knew, or the first Christians, we are at least middle-aged, and our body of knowledge is light years from theirs. Should the church remain forever pledged to the old knowledge, the former understanding, and not keep abreast of developments in every field? Is this why so many Christians renounce Darwin and thoughts of evolution? Why they want nothing to do with Freud and Jung and Adler? Why they have no use for stem-cell research, black holes in space, and the mysteries of DNA?

Sometimes I am enthralled at the miracle of my own body and its complex environment. I contemplate the billions of neurons in my brain and the thousands of tendrils waving out from each of them, like minute ghostly arms, attempting to touch, form connections, however tenuous, with the tendrils from other neurons, and, when they manage it, altering the state of my consciousness ever so slightly, with trillions and quadrillions of possible states available to them, so that I am an almost infinite hotbed of possibilities, I alone, in my own mind. Say I am sitting on a park bench looking at the stars, and my mind is actively engaged at making those connections, so that I shall hear music or imagine drama or begin to compose a poem, and the realization strikes me, in the midst of this cauldron of shifting thoughts and understandings, that I myself am only one of billions of human beings regarding the same stars. Isn't it thrilling beyond words?! Doesn't it invoke in me a sense of reverence for creation and its Maker that I couldn't have attained had I not known something of the brain that wasn't revealed to worshipers before the twentieth century?

I resonate to Redfield, Murphy, and Timbers's *God and the Evolving Universe* when they talk about the extraordinary capacities some human beings develop to "sense" and "know" things of which the rest of us remain totally unaware: wine tasters who can discriminate among thousands of vintages; "cloth feelers" who can discern even slight differences in textures or weaves; clairvoyants who are sensitive to invisible leadings; athletes who can spot sudden movements, openings, opportunities; bush hunters who can spy small game a mile away; meditationists who sense the inner workings of their own bodies; and musicians who are able to hear intricacies of sound that ordinary persons miss.[5]

Most of us live our entire lives without developing a single sense to the point where it detects things not perceived by everybody else. It never occurs to us that there are depths and depths to the mysteries of the universe, and that if we could only train ourselves adequately, and were passionate about doing so, we could become attuned to far more than we presently know or perceive. Think about the musicians who say, when they are composing, that the music already existed and they only tuned into it, and the writers of both fiction and nonfiction who testify that they tapped into something in their unconscious that simply dictated

5. Redfield, Murphy, and Timbers, *God and the Evolving Universe*, 81–95.

what they were to write. Picasso said once that his paintings already existed in eternity, and all he had to do was concentrate and enable them to take shape on his canvases. How much of our potential brain power do we use to accomplish anything we do? Ten percent? Twenty? What if we learned to operate at full capacity, or even half capacity? Then what would the world look like to us?

Of course new knowledge and understanding challenge old conceptions of God and the universe. Of course they call into question scriptures and creeds and outdated theologies. But isn't that in itself proof that God is a *living* God, a dynamic Creator, that God is not some static old fool with a long beard bemoaning the fact that his creation didn't come off without some hitches in the beginning, so that Adam and Eve managed to screw up the paradise he had in mind, but is a God always in the process of becoming and making and, yes, loving?

Take the concept known as the "butterfly effect," that the settling of a butterfly on a blossom in one part of the world sets off reactions in other parts, even an earthquake or a tidal wave if the effect is just right. The preacher cries "Foolish! Everything is predetermined in the mind of God!" But what if the chain of events triggered by the butterfly is a microscopic part of an elaborate scheme, so that God's foreknowledge is far more complicated than we ever imagined, mysteries upon mysteries upon mysteries? Just as chaos theory renders Calvin's *Institutes* and their belabored exposition of the doctrine of predestination as limited and silly as a bit of doggerel spouted by a man in his cups, all science begs us to step up to new discoveries and formulations more commensurate with the size of the expanded multiverses we now know to be God's true domain, and not continue to wallow in a pint-sized puddle beside the ocean.

"No," cries the fundamentalist, the traditionalist, the evangelical, even the cowardly moderate, "we cannot go there! It is too great a leap from where we are, and too much may be lost in the going." It is a gamble few seem willing to take. Better stay where we are, in a small corner of the cave, than venture forth into a larger world and risk losing a handle on truth as we have understood it.

Surely we are nearing the tipping point, though, where more and more will take the risk. If they don't—if they continue to cling to archaic creeds and old mythologies—then the cleavage between religion and science can only continue to grow, and at an exponential rate. We are already traveling apart.

Getting Past Our Christology

Dare I say this, that more than anything else it is our Christology that makes us timid about going forward? Suppose we found the courage to own a world vaster and more mysterious than the one we knew, what would be the result of that for our views of Jesus and his work of redemption? Might it not turn the telescope around so that we had to view him, not as the pantocrator Christ, the preexistent deity without whom not even our pitiable little world was created, but suddenly in minuscule as the humbler Jesus of the synoptic Gospels, before the church magnified his role to portray him as "very God of very God"?

What happens, for example, to the lordship of Christ when we look beyond this tiny planet of ours and consider that there may be life in other galaxies, albeit of very different sorts from our own? Would he still be Lord of Lords and King of Kings? Remember St. John's paean:

> Then I heard every creature in heaven and on earth and under
> the earth and in the sea, and all that is in them, singing,
>> "To the one seated on the throne and to the Lamb
>> be blessing and honor and glory and might
>> forever and ever!" (Rev 5:13)

What would become of such adoration, which is now woven into the creeds and hymnody and theology of the church? Can it possibly be shelved and all but forgotten in a new theology of the creation in which Jesus is only one of the sons of men and not the deified Son of God we meet in the writings of St. Paul and other Christian myth-makers? Or must it somehow be subsumed under what Matthew Fox has called "the Cosmic Christ,"⁶ whose being joined together with the historical Jesus, he says, is the only thing that will at last make Christianity whole? Either way, it means taking giant strides beyond the simple, literalistic figure most Christians worship today.

Diarmuid O'Murchu, the Irish Catholic priest, may offer a valid middle way. He talks, in both *Quantum Theology* and *Catching Up with Jesus*, about a "relational matrix" that transcends all arguments about both science and Christology. The matrix, he says, is what Jesus's entire ministry was about, not about powers and authorities and being set above all that is, but about "a world of unconditional love" to which Jesus invites his followers in every age, and beside which all ethical and theological questions become moot.

In a section of *Catching Up with Jesus* centering on resurrection, which O'Murchu sees as the seminal problem and at the same time the connection between science and religion, he has his Jesus say:

> That I was risen from the dead became the new myth. Fascinating, intriguing, and quite bombastic at times. For me and my relational matrix there is no distinction between the realm of the dead and that of the living. Creation is one unbroken continuum: the dead and the living share the same living space, but at different vibrational levels.
>
> The realm of the dead is not some distant sphere to which one escapes, or from which one is "risen." My relational matrix inhabits both, and so does every living creature in potential

6. See Fox, *The Coming of the Cosmic Christ*.

form. My resurrected state is supposed to be one in which I am more real than I was in my earthly indwelling. It is more enduring, yes, but not more real. It could not be more real than my relational matrix, from which all relationality emanates, and relationality is the basis of everything in creation including what you Christians call "resurrection."

Again, Christians have this strange preoccupation with trying to prove my divinity, and I guess they consider resurrection a necessary prerequisite to substantiate that "proof." I find the whole thing a bit repugnant; it does not even make for good fiction and has proved to be a massive distraction from the things that really matter. You humans have not even come to terms with my humanity, so how could you make any sense of my divinity!

Anyhow, as I said previously, I am not worried about my divinity, and I see no reason why you should either. If you took my humanity seriously, you wouldn't have any problem with understanding my divinity, and you would quickly come to realize that resurrection is about a fuller flowering of my humanity at the service of the New Reign, rather than anything to do with proof of my divinity.

The problem with you humans is that you don't stay grounded, close to earth, your primordial womb, close to creation, the primary revelation of my relational matrix. You waste so much precious time and energy fleeing in the realms of "divine" fantasy, trying to transcend to the heavenly realm in some nonexistent outer sphere. Stop deluding yourselves. There is one creation, one universe, the unfolding tapestry of my relational matrix. That is your true home, in life, in death, and beyond death. Creation itself is forever undergoing the process of resurrection-transformation. I had to undergo it, and so do you. Resurrection is not just about me, it is about all of us and also about the whole of creation, planetary and cosmic alike.

Now that is something else the scripture scholars did not get right. They developed these so-called resurrection appearances. Good stories, I agree, but rather misleading. From the Christian point of view, resurrection is not so much about me as about my followers. Resurrection is the hope that defies all hopelessness. It is the power from within that kept my followers faithful to the dream after the authorities got rid of me. Resurrection is that intuitive conviction that the dream of my relational matrix has not been subverted by my individual death and that, paradoxically, it is even more resilient because of it.[7]

Who can hear such music? Not many mainstream Christians, I expect. It sounds far more like heresy than Christian doctrine. Yet it may well be the most Christian thing any of us is likely to read this year or ever, for it is couched in an imagination that is the only way of making sense of the tension between Christianity and the scientific worldview now predominant in our culture. Is it 100 percent accurate? Of course not. Is the Apostles' Creed? The Pledge of Allegiance? "The Star-Spangled Banner"? It is like all creeds, a glorious, impudent dare flung against the canopy of the heavens, or, more specifically, against the gray expanse of our mental powers. It isn't meant to be tried for its ABCs but for its magic, its power to transport the soul, its gift for helping us understand what it means to be followers of Jesus in a changing world. And, given the fact that we live in an age when cultures are in rapid transition, it is a good pattern for reconceiving our faith, because it both acknowledges the Christian narrative—whence we have come—and the growing body of scientific knowledge that stands at odds with all ancient theologies.

The Father Too

But Christology isn't the only major area of doctrine affected by Christianity's clash with modern culture. Patrology too is assaulted. What does it mean to say that God is our Father, as most of us have done since childhood? "Our Father, who art in heaven" is almost as rooted in our subliminal minds as "Mama" and "Dada." Even many feminists, who often balk at patriarchal language in general, confess that in the privacy of their own hearts they still find the word "Father" forming surreptitiously on their tongues.

7. O'Murchu, *Catching Up with Jesus*, 162–63.

Yet which of us, as modern human beings, doesn't hesitate at least ever so slightly over that nomenclature today because we remember that it had its historical origin in a religion centered in Israel and Judea and is thus in some vague, indefinable way to be discounted by its moorings in a prescientific past? What it expresses as a familiarizing term for the Hebraic deity who thundered from Mount Sinai is surely tender and touching. But we who live in the twenty-first century are mindful of vast universes beyond the pastoral world of Jesus's day, of quarks and black holes and dying stars, and some of us cannot repeat the word without having some slight shadow cross the threshold of consciousness to remind us of our new positions in a world where, as journalists remind us, cosmology is rapidly replacing theology.

Robert Wuthnow, the sociologist, complains in *Christianity in the 21st Century* that one of the primary challenges facing the church in our time is that "it has often robbed itself of the authority to tell its stories." Beguiled by a compulsion to appear sophisticated and up-to-date, it has talked in scientific, historical, and theological terms instead of relating its own signature stories.[8] Wuthnow doesn't spell out exactly what these stories are, but one assumes they are the narratives involving Moses and the Holy Land, Jonah and the great fish, Jesus and his ministry of teaching and healing, and, climactically, the resurrection of Jesus and the formation of the early church.

Perhaps Wuthnow and I do not travel in the same circles, but I have not run into many ministers who hesitate to tell the old stories. In my own opinion, the rub seems to come when there is little apparent connectedness between those stories and the new story, the story of our expanding universe and a growing body of scientific evidence that contradicts the Bible's more naive accounts of time, the universe, and God's authority to preside over them, so that an increasing number of thoughtful Christians no longer find

8. Wuthnow, *Christianity in the 21st Century*, 48.

hymns and sermons credible in the way they once were. There is an almost indefinable something missing in them, and it may be their ministers' inability to create linkages between them and what we are seeing and feeling now that we inhabit a more scientifically based and empirically conscious culture. That is, the fault is not in the difference between the two ways of regarding the world, but in those who are commissioned to interpret from one world to the other, who are ordained to "explain" the dis-ease we experience in attempting to straddle dueling points of view.

Take the matter of prayer, for example, which for most Christians today immediately opens Pandora's box. (I almost said "the *simple* matter of prayer," but hesitated because there is nothing at all simple about it.) Most of us still pray, if not regularly, at least whenever we come under undue stress or face an extreme situation, such as the serious illness of a loved one. Yet we would hardly be citizens of an empirical world order if we did not also wonder about the real efficacy of prayer—whether God does indeed hear and answer prayer, or, for that matter, whether God even exists, and, if so, is capable of responding to our petitions.

Sometimes we take refuge in the stories of friends, or even from our own past, of times when God did seem to answer prayer and save a loved one from dying or prevent a flood from sweeping away a town. Even then, however, we are plagued by a certain amount of doubt, wondering whether the loved one's recovery or the town's averting danger could be owed merely to chance. For we can cite many instances in which we or others prayed fervently for a particular outcome that didn't occur, and we or they had to be reminded to add that little escape clause, "Not my will, but thine, be done."

John Calvin of course talked about the *inscrutability* of the sovereign divinity's will. It is a fine dodge, or was, in a time when most people lived under despots whose inscrutability was part of their mystique as powerful rulers. But now, in a gentler, kinder time, when even great rulers are expected to "have a heart" and be moved by the imprecations of their subjects, it doesn't do much for the divine image to talk about "a higher wisdom" that led God to answer prayer by saying no in order to achieve some hidden aim as yet undisclosed to us human beings.

Most Christians appear to be greatly encouraged by the latest findings of some scientific experiment that claims to have proved in even a minimal way that prayer is efficacious to the growth of plants—"the ones prayed over grew two inches higher than the ones not prayed over"—or enables religious persons to be more content and thus to live longer than another test group with no pretensions to faith. I'm afraid this only bespeaks our eagerness to have our religion validated by modern science, and, conversely, a deficiency of confidence in it when the validation is not present.

My point is that exponents of religious belief are today in the awkward position of trying to straddle two realms, that of faith and that of scientific knowledge, and one of the reasons many feel that we have outgrown the church is that our leaders, both teachers and preachers, do not face the situation honestly, but try to avoid it completely or to cover it over with occasional winks and nods toward the scientific worldview, as if they were perfectly comfortable co-existing with them in a world where the two would be completely harmonious if only we had a better language for expressing their agreement.

For myself, I am tired of skirting the issue and believe it is high time our theologians and preachers talked more straightfor-wardly about the clash of religion and science and how we must amend our religious views in order to go on living in a world of real facts.

Years ago, in his novel *The Mackerel Plaza*, Peter de Vries described a liberal church in Connecticut where the pulpit was constructed of "four distinctly varying hues of fruitwood to symbolize the failure of the Gospels to harmonize."[9] I remember, when I read this—it was sometime in the 1960s—that I applauded de Vries's honesty and forthrightness and decided it was high time every church in America acquired such a pulpit. Now I think it is high time we begin to assess our situation more courageously and, instead of trying to return to first-century Christianity as many churches proudly proclaim they are trying to do, march bravely onward to develop new theologies that somehow embrace both the general principles of our ancient faith and the brilliant discoveries of our present science.

This might well mean discarding numerous ideas and images from our past, but there is little point in attempting to preserve them in the face of contrary evidence from researchers and mathematicians in our own day. I have always appreciated Picasso's statement that he didn't mind painting out a color because, if it was any good, it would come back. I am confident that the same is true of any Judeo-Christian ideas or values we might surrender now: if they are any good, if they are transcendentally and everlastingly true, they will always come back, regardless of how many times we have overlooked or attempted to expunge them.

St. Paul said in his letter to the Galatians that the law was only a pedagogue or school teacher to bring us to Christ (Gal 3:24). That is, in an image known to most Greek and Roman Christians of the time, the law was the slave to whom were entrusted the freed man's children while they were being raised to the point where they could make personal decisions and thus become truly free. To be in Christ—if we follow his analogy to the end—meant to be free, to be no longer bound to the rules and expectations of the school master, who was discardable once the children had reached a certain stage of maturity.

Can't the same image or metaphor be instructive in our present situation? What we were taught by our forebears in the

9. De Vries, *The Mackerel Plaza*, 10.

faith—the rudiments of Judaism and Christianity, as expressed in the Ten Commandments, the Beatitudes, and the teachings of the church about Jesus's death and resurrection—was our school master to bring us to our present level of understanding. Some of us are now mature enough to renounce the school master and move on to a new and freer level of thought and understanding. It is for this new level that the tutelage of the school master existed. For that, we shall always be beholden to the school master. But now it is time for us to spread our wings and fly, to take what we have learned and absorbed, and, facing a new world of science and philosophy, move on to the creation of new metaphors and combinations of knowledge that will satisfy us more fully until an even higher level of comprehension is attained, at which time the act of freeing ourselves should occur all over again.

Once more, it is to Diarmuid O'Murchu I turn for his elegant way of expressing what I am trying to say. In *Quantum Theology* he discusses quantum physics, the idea that literally everything in the universe contains little packets of energy, which Einstein called *quanta*, and that there is nothing, even in the stones in the riverbeds and the desk on which my computer sits, that is not filled with constituents which, if we could only see them more microscopically, are teeming with life and energy. Our Christianity derives from a more prosaic, hard-headed view of reality, the one demonstrated by Dr. Johnson when he kicked a rock and said, "Thus I refute Berkeley!"—Bishop Berkeley being the eminent proponent of a Platonic or idealistic view of the world. But the knowledge that the world is not the way we thought it was, but is always in constant motion and evolution toward some new state of being, obliges us to think of God as being much more totally and intimately involved in creation than we once believed.

What is more, we ourselves are much more involved in creation than we once believed. In our former worldview, that of Newtonian physics, we assumed that the observer of everything stood outside the field of change and evolution, and was merely a spectator. But now, in the world of quantum physics, we understand otherwise. The observer is not only involved in what is observed but actually makes a difference in what is happening. What we bring to the observation of things actually influences what we are observing, so that together we are in the process of creating new realities all the time. We prejudice the outcome by even talking about the subject.

Thus, claims O'Murchu,

> Reclaiming our spiritual identity is not a case of becoming religious again, going to church on Sunday, following the rules and laws of a particular faith, reading the Bible or Koran everyday. No, it goes much deeper than any of this. As many of the great faiths suggest (but poorly implement) spirituality is about enlightenment and liberation. The spiritual journey is about opening up new horizons of love and understanding, not by ignoring or bypassing the darkness and pain of life, but precisely through experiencing and integrating them. Through this process we are liberated from the confines, restrictions, and limitations imposed on us frequently by our own personal ignorance, but also by the collective oppression of our man-made institutions.[10]

It is in light of this explanation that we can better grasp what O'Murchu's Jesus meant by the "relational matrix" in his later book, *Catching Up with Jesus*. For he goes on to say (in *Quantum Theology*), "Everything is created out of relatedness, sustained through relationships, and thrives on interdependence."[11] Quantum theology, in other words, provides a new, more fluid structure within which we can understand the relationship between the old faith and the new, the ancient patriarchal world and the world of twenty-first century physics, biology, and psychology.

10. O'Murchu, *Quantum Theology*, 77.
11. O'Murchu, ibid., 80.

Personally, I find this very promising and exciting. Being neither a physicist nor a mathematician, I know there is much about modern science that I shall never comprehend. But what I do understand is that I needed a new template with which to explore my faith and its relationship to the universe, and this provides it in a way the old template did not.

It doesn't explain everything, of course. But it points me to a way into the wilderness that I can now take. As John Pokinghorne, the theoretical physicist who became an Anglican priest, said in *Quarks, Chaos, and Christianity*, we don't have to have a perfect map in order to begin our journey; we can use one that is still quite sketchy and vague, so long as it establishes some useful points of reference. Later, when we know more about the territory we are exploring, we can fill in additional details. Meanwhile, we can go on warily and with a sense of assurance in the direction open to us, comforted by the general correctness of what we do know.

Maybe someday the church will lurch forward over this formidable hump it seems to have got caught on and find itself in a real Wonderland, reimagining what it is to be church in a time of rapid global transition. Perhaps there will even arise some more theologians like O'Murchu who will not fear to breach the wilderness with new books about being truly Christian in an age of scientific advance. I had dinner recently with some young religion professors and asked who they thought are the real theologians coming along today. I was stunned to find that they couldn't offer a single name of anyone who may one day stand among them with the stature of a Karl Barth, a Paul Tillich, or a Reinhold Niebuhr. When I asked if they read O'Murchu, they stared at me and asked, "Who's he?"

This suggests that part of our problem is that, with all the emphasis on social change in the past few decades—especially in the areas of feminism and homosexuality—seminaries haven't been producing many theologians eager to deal with issues of religion and science. I find that regrettable, but know it is possible I've overlooked some fine young theologians because they simply haven't yet made their mark.

Meanwhile, until they do, I close this chapter with a heartfelt prayer from William Cleary's *Prayers to An Evolutionary God*, which I believe is a fine expression of what I've been attempting to say:

> Boundless Sea of Love and Energy,
> > our future and our God,
> may all your dreams for us come true:
> > your steady, motherlike imaginings,
> > > and your fatherly hopes,
> your creative purposes evident everywhere
> > in the world.
> Guide us to our truest selves,
> > co-creators with you of this environment.
> Persuade us to be worthy inheritors
> > of the astonishing evolving reality
> > > in which we live:
> > appreciators of the daytime in all its
> > > colors and aromas,
> > admirers of the heavens at night,
> > reverent caretakers of our generous
> > > green earth,
> > respectful of everything alive—
> > especially of our fellow humans
> > > in all their bewildering diversity.
> May it be so.[12]

12. Cleary, *Prayers to an Evolutionary God*, 7.

7

The Church's Lack of Imagination—or Spirit!

The Church historically has been willing to criticize, marginalize, or even expel its most creative thinkers.

—JOHN SHELBY SPONG, *WHY CHRISTIANITY MUST CHANGE OR DIE*[1]

What would happen if churches, synagogues, and mosques underwent a time of verbal fasting, when they put their old stories and traditional religious languages on hiatus? At first things would probably get worse. People wouldn't know how to talk about religious matters. But gradually congregations would begin to experiment with new metaphors and create a new poetry of faith by sharing stories and by helping one another discover fresh expressions of their perennial fears and hopes.

—SAM KEEN, *IN THE ABSENCE OF GOD*[2]

The Cosmic Christ and the living cosmology that the Cosmic Christ ushers into society and psyche have the power to launch an era of what I call deep ecumenism. Deep ecumenism is the movement that will unleash the wisdom

1. Spong, *Why Christianity Must Change or Die*, 4–5.
2. Keen, *In the Absence of God*, 53.

of all world religions—Hinduism and Buddhism, Islam and Judaism, Taoism and Shintoism, Christianity in all its forms, and native religions and goddess religions throughout the world. This unleashing of wisdom holds the last hope for the survival of the planet we call home.

—MATTHEW FOX, *THE COMING OF THE COSMIC CHRIST*[3]

Religious life is changing before our eyes. We have no idea what forms it will take . . . Yet there is no other path but paralysis and death. Many of our spiritual traditions will survive the transition. Some probably will not. We need not be afraid: we must cross the bridge and aim for the other shore.

—NILES ELLIOT GOLDSTEIN, *GOD AT THE EDGE*[4]

Alvin Toffler was right about future shock. Everything changes so fast now that we can't begin to keep up with it. It's hard to remember what life was like before computers. Now practically everything that touches our lives—banking, shopping, designing, publishing, travel, office work, climate control, music, art, entertainment, communication, medical service—is drastically affected by their existence.

Sociologists say they are changing us as much as we are changing them. There is a symbiotic relationship between us and the technology of the computer that actually alters our brains and the way we think.

Who could have predicted that the world would shrink so quickly? Globalism is no longer a threat, it's a fact of life. We wake up on bedding woven in China, enjoy orange juice from

3. Fox, *The Coming of the Cosmic Christ*, 228.
4. Goldstein, *God at the Edge*, 186.

Guatemala and coffee from Brazil, don clothing designed in Paris and assembled in Bulgaria, drive to work in a Japanese car, sit at a desk imported from Korea, talk on a phone made in Taiwan to people in Germany, Singapore, and Zimbabwe, have dinner at an Indian restaurant, enjoy wine from Australia followed by coffee from Borneo, and retire to our homes to watch a British TV program filmed in Peru.

There are still some kinks to work out, but we are much more of a world family than anybody fifty years ago would have guessed.

In every previous cultural revolution since the time of Jesus, Christians have been in the forefront, not only adapting theologies and liturgies to fit it but actually driving it, shaping it, and proclaiming the gospel through its exciting new contours. Think Augustine and his influence on the Middle Ages. Think Luther, Calvin, and Zwingli and the Reformation. Think John Wesley and the Methodist revolution. Think the American church and the shaping of our nation.

But not this time.

This time the church appears to be sitting things out on the sideline. The revolution we're going through now—the biggest since the end of the Middle Ages—has caught us by surprise. Instead of generating and shaping it, the church has been beaten and battered by it. We are like surfers who weren't up to the magnitude of the waves, and they have wiped us out.

Oh, we can point to the megachurches and pretend they are the wave of the future in ecclesiastical sociology. Maybe they are. They appear to be the way the church intends to survive into the middle of this century and beyond, by jettisoning as much denominational baggage as possible, dumping a lot of old doctrinal fussiness, and offering a smorgasbord of classes and seminars to attract everybody from three-year-olds to centenarians. It is entrepreneurialism. Twentieth-century Christianity dumbed down for the masses.

But, to tell the truth, big one-size-fits-all churches don't exhibit much imagination, do they? They haven't come up with much of anything really new. They've only borrowed the bits and pieces of theology and liturgy they thought would work, without inventing anything that wasn't there before. They don't produce theologians, the way the old denominations did. Their preachers are primarily sanctified motivational speakers who know how to caress a microphone and impart a measure of psychic comfort to their audiences. They are sort of like field hospitals to treat shell-shocked folks who wander in from a hard week's work and the general desperation of suburban life.

Let's be honest, there isn't a lot of imagination in the church these days, is there? Real imagination, that is able to combine previously unlinked elements and produce a truly new entity. Imagination that soars even in tiny spaces and concocts revolutionary ideas and objects. Imagination that operates in the most arid climates to create a rain forest or a hot shower or a cold beer. Imagination that dreams whole new worlds out of practically nothing, and conjures wild hares out of worn-out hats.

The early Christians had imagination. Boy, did they have it! Somehow they managed to parlay the death of their leader on a cross into a big Pentecostal meeting in Jerusalem and then to a worldwide network of eager new witnesses and theologians. Of course they had the resurrection to work with. That was pretty cool. In fact, it was the most fantastic revolutionary happening in the history of the world. But to their credit, they didn't get in its way. They learned to handle it like a fire hose, so that the power was directed where they wanted it to go, without wiping them out in the process.

Think what they did, those early Christians. They invented new liturgies, new creeds, new hymns, new literary forms, new sacraments, new apocalypses, new ways of communicating, new theologies, and, when they had converted the Roman emperor to their side, new architecture and another round of new liturgies, new music, and new oratory. We could even say they imagined a whole new world, because they changed the way history was made, viewed, and recorded.

By comparison, ours is a dull, listless, backward generation incapable of making anything new or exciting. Instead of remolding the faith for our time and a few centuries to come, which should be our immediate calling in an age of transition like this one, we merely continue to limp along with the models and patterns left over from a more creative past.[5]

I was thinking about this recently when we took some house guests into Washington, DC, to worship at the National Cathedral. We went early so our guests could prowl around the sanctuary, taking photographs of the brilliant windows. When we finally sat down to await the beginning of the service, one of our friends, who had never traveled overseas, turned and asked, "How does this compare with British and European Cathedrals you've visited?"

The question momentarily discombobulated me.

"Well, it's certainly large," I said as I tried to organize my answer. "But not terribly large by the standards of Westminster Abbey or Notre Dame."

Then, before I knew it, I found myself speaking from my heart.

"You know, the thing your question makes me realize about this place," I said, "is that it is so imitative. I mean, I can't help contrasting it with Coventry Cathedral in England, for example."

5. Brian McLaren bemoans this in *A New Kind of Christian*, when Neo Oliver, one of the two characters in dialogue, writes to the other, Reverend Dan Poole, "In [my] dream [last night], you were exhausted and worn to the bone, struggling to shape a church that was meaningfully expressing the gospel in this new world we've been talking about. I asked God why you were so tired, and this answer came to me: there are so few working at this exploration of faith in postmodern territory, and all of those are exhausted because it is so difficult" (138).

I explained about the old cathedral that was bombed by the Germans in World War II, and how members saved parts of it but then erected a new, modern cathedral next to it, with its entryway through an immense glass wall by John Hutton with translucent etchings of saints and angels abounding on it.

"I wish the people who planned this cathedral," I continued, "had been as daring and innovative as Sir Basil Spence, who designed the new Coventry Cathedral. When I think of the brilliance of that building, and how perfectly it expresses the contemporary spirit, I feel rather sad about this one, that is so completely and woefully like most of the old medieval cathedrals."

I tried to describe Graham Sutherland's enormous tapestry in the chancel, with its bold, modern shade of green and jarring depiction of Christ in glory, holding man between his feet, and the stunning floor-to-ceiling window in the south wall by John Piper and Patrick Reyntiens, as grand and eye-catching as the sun itself, framing a magnificent sandstone boulder from Barakat, outside Bethlehem, with a baptismal font scooped in its top.

If the service hadn't commenced at this point, I would have told him also about the haunting little Chapel of Christ in Gethsemane, whose entry is encircled by a wrought-iron reminder of the crown of thorns, and the circular Chapel of Industry, with walls of plain glass looking out onto the industrial sites of Coventry, which were the primary objects of the Nazi bombings.

Conceptually, Coventry Cathedral belongs to modern times, not to the Middle Ages, and makes our spirits soar not only because of the heroic story of its members during the war but because it *is* contemporary and makes a dramatic statement about life and art at the time when it was built. National Cathedral, on the other hand, is an architectural contretemps. It may sit on the most commanding site in the District of Columbia and offer a dignified setting for state funerals and military services, but it is nevertheless a monument to what *was*, not what is or is yet to come. It is what Scrooge would have visited with his first guide, not with the second or third.

The same goes for most churches today. They are monuments to the past, not the present. They disappoint us because they don't soar into the future and remind us that God is still alive and still creating the world. Their theology is retrospective, not prospective. Their educational systems remain rooted in nineteenth- and twentieth-century pedagogy. Their hymnody is largely derivative from the grand old hymns of the eighteenth and nineteenth centuries. Their rhetoric is either antique and stilted or cheaply modern and inarticulate. Their art is clonic and deadly. Their imagination is leaden and heavy, rarely lilting and playful.

Getting Over What We've Already Experienced

One of my favorite parables is from Clyde Reid's book *Celebrate the Temporary*.[6] Reid was a sensitivity-training guru in the 1970s, and was holding a workshop at a retreat center in Colorado. It was not going well, because one of the participants kept recalling an outstanding group he had belonged to in the past and the leader of that group, whom he described as brilliant and exciting. Regardless of what Reid or other participants did or said, he derailed everything by interjecting memories of the great experiences he had in that former group. Reid said he was on the verge of canceling the weekend and refunding everybody's money.

Then he had an idea.

Summoning the man to the front of the group, he threw him an imaginary shovel. Having gone through role-playing before, the man "caught" it.

"Now," said Reid, "I want you to dig a hole."

---

6. Reid, *Celebrate the Temporary*, 56–57.

The man commenced the imaginary digging, happy to be front and center in the group.

"Make it a little deeper," said Reid. "Also a little longer."

The man went on digging.

"Now," said Reid, when the man had labored for a while, "let me explain what we're going to do. What you've been digging is a grave. We're all going to gather around this grave and have an interment service."

The man looked puzzled.

"What we're going to bury in this grave," Reid continued, "is your old group leader and your old group experience."

And they did. They went through a little ritual as if it were a real graveside service. And when they had finished, Reid handed the man the imaginary shovel again and ordered him to fill up the hole.

By this time, the man was quite excited about what he was doing. He had become the center of attention, which is probably what he wanted all along. This group became the greatest group he had ever been a part of, and Clyde Reid became the greatest group leader he had ever known. And some other group leader was going to have to deal with him somewhere down the road.

When I first read this story, I began thinking about my own life and how I had spent years looking for religious experiences that would replicate the ones I had found so exciting in my youth. None ever did.

"How many experiences in my life have been so great," I asked myself, "that I have enshrined them and made it hard to have other experiences? How many of my great religious adventures have actually stood in the way of my having more?"

Now I am asking the same about the church and its tendency to fasten on great moments in its history, turning them into such monuments of grace and glory that it fails to see the multiple possibilities of new moments it could be having. We are all human, of course, and tend to idolize the noblest or most exciting events in our past. But the moment we do that we blind ourselves to the potential for events that might even surpass the former ones.

This is why there is a saying, "If you meet the Buddha in the road, kill him." It isn't out of disrespect for the Buddha and what he brought to hundreds of millions of Buddhists. It is an acknowledgement of Buddha's own teaching that nothing—not anything in the world, even Buddha himself—should ever come to stand in the way of one's continuing enlightenment.

Think for a moment what it would mean for the church to adopt such a principle. We would no longer build all our church buildings to look like all the other church buildings in the world. We wouldn't go on worshiping in the same old patterns. We wouldn't recite the same creeds and dogmatic truths. We would find ourselves suddenly free to be Christians in our own way and in our own time.

We could never start completely *de novo*, of course, for we can never empty our minds and hearts of all the things stored in them from the time we were born. But we would essentially discover a new freedom to rearrange things, to use the old building blocks in new ways, to create buildings and hymns and patterns of thought in our own way.

Our problem is our fear of heresy, of being caught off base in our thoughts and ideas, our ways of expressing the faith. Our fear makes us like processionary caterpillars, those amusing insects that follow one another without any thought for what they are doing. Placed on the lip of a fruit jar, they will lock onto one another and go around in circles for hours, until they fall off from starvation and exhaustion.

Pope Benedict XVI, unfortunately, seemed to be a processionary pope. In 2007, he reiterated his own earlier statement that the Roman Catholic Church is the only way of salvation because it is the only church directly descended from St. Peter. Imagine all those caterpillars following one another from our own era back to the time of the early church, and never suspecting there could be any saving grace outside their own conga line. How sad. How exclusivist. And how severely such a viewpoint limits the power of God in the world![7]

But Catholics have no lock on traditionalism. Any church that has been in existence thirty years or longer is victimized by its own institutionalism—the history of what a previous generation said or believed. And fundamentalism is a beautiful example of being bound to the past, chained to it as if by virtual bonds. It doesn't go back to the Bible, as its adherents like to insist, but only to the great old Bible conferences of the late nineteenth and early twentieth centuries, when the lions of conservatism throve on attacking Darwin and eventually developed a list of the "fundamental" beliefs to which they insisted all true Christians must adhere. Still, they have exhibited a lock-step mentality second to none and burned many an accused heretic at their imaginary stakes for exhibiting the least sign of deviation from their militant dogmas.

None of these insecure and unimaginative Christians ever take an honest look at the early church, where there was an absolute plethora of doctrines, methods, and understandings of what Christianity was about. We understand this today, when we are viewing the tip of the iceberg in all the newly discovered Gospels and collateral writings from that era and can only imagine how scattered and unregulated both theology and practice were among the thousands of Christian communities in the lands around the Mediterranean. The conservative members of the church are fearful of getting into that Pandora's box. They want to contain all the

---

7. David Gibson, a committed Roman Catholic reporter and journalist, says in his book *The Coming Catholic Church* that the real hope for Catholics lies with the more innovative Americans who refuse to let Rome have the last word. He also cautions that "the first task before Catholics is to figure out what to preserve and what to jettison—what is essential and what is peripheral" (343).

new information, to suppress it, even to eradicate the evidence, so they can go on pretending that everything was as monolithic in the beginning as they insist it must be today.

Think of the efforts conservative scholars have made to harmonize the Gospels and convince us that Mark, Luke, Matthew, and John all said the same things, even though their interpretations and emphases were at times wildly divergent. And they do the same thing with science and religion, trying to stuff Darwinism back in the bag the same way they did Copernicanism and all the other great moments of discovery in the history of what we have found out about our world.

If they can't deny something because it is too self-evident and popular, then they try to harmonize it, to find ways of taking the edge off the difference between the Bible and modern science so that the Bible is still regarded as completely true in every respect. They cannot bear to think of a world where their precious scriptures are at odds with the truth.

We can see the same harmonizing rage in the Christian book industry of our time, and, through it, popular Christianity as a whole. Any author of religious books knows how strictly the CBA, or Christian Booksellers Association, has guarded its shelves against publications that don't hew slavishly to their doctrinal standards.

A few years ago, a well-known denominational house was preparing a manuscript of mine for publication. I was appalled at the blue-penciling job a young, relatively inexperienced editor had performed on it. When I asked what was wrong with a number of references that had been excluded—to Judaism, Zen Buddhism, Carl Jung, and *One Flew Over the Cuckoo's Nest*, among others—she said she was only following the house's new rules to bring their books into conformity with "CBA expectations." Apparently the CBA was guarding its readers against the very mention of certain names or ideas that might corrupt them.

Every book it admitted into its stores had to be homogenized and sanitized before it got there.

What do these people fear? That God and Christ and the church cannot stand divergency? That they must be protected like old antimacassars under glass because they are too fragile to be exposed to light or handled like other persons and ideas? Such an attitude is an insult to the very nature of God as creator of the universe and to Christ as the great liberator.

It is all about control, I think. They want to control how people think about God, Christ, and church, how they express themselves, lest everything spin off in hopelessly diverse directions. They are like the Grand Inquisitor in Dostoevsky's story, who doesn't want Christ returning to Seville during the Inquisition because he will upset the balance of everything and they will no longer be in charge of it all. They want only the God of their design, the Christ of their limited understanding, the church of their own schemings, and not the real ones, that are effervescent and explosive and—unmanageable.

If I were in charge of the church, God forbid, I'd convene a world council of the most talented, fantastic artists, musicians, writers, and architects, including as many rebels as possible, and charge them with reimagining the church for our age and the one to come. I'd say: "Go to it, you lot. Talk, dream, argue with one another, be preposterous, let your imaginations range over everything, soar like eagles, dip like kites, and come up with thousands of ideas for a richer, deeper community of believers, a broader diversity of propositions and doctrines, more fantastic ways of expressing ourselves in worship, an incredible array of ways for applying ourselves to the solution of worldwide human problems, incredible new architecture for our buildings, or maybe even ways of subsisting without buildings. In other words, pull out all the stops, reconceive who we are and how we could be in the next century, so that we don't merely replicate our highly questionable past but exist in the present as spot-on candidates for the kingdom of God!"

I don't know all the new artists, writers, and thinkers, but if I had been convening such a conference a few years ago, when they were all alive, I'd have wanted Beckett and Ionesco and Picasso and Strindberg and Tom Stoppard and Andrew Lloyd-Webber and Martha Graham and Buckminster Fuller and I. M. Pei and Eleanor Roosevelt and Duke Ellington and Kurt Vonnegut and Matisse and Michelangelo Antonioni and Stephen Hawking and D. T. Suzuki and Doug Marlette and Will Campbell and Flannery O'Connor and John Cage and Walt Disney and Ken Kesey and Harvey Cox and Alan Watts and Jacques Cousteau and James Redfield and Mahatma Gandhi and Martin Luther King Jr. and James Hillman and Eliel Saarinen and Steve Jobs and Molly Ivins and Peter de Vries and Fannie Flagg and James Lovelock and Annie Dillard and Peter Shaffer and Nikos Kazantzakis, and now I'd be sure to include Joseph Girzone, whose Joshua novels are filled with the disguised radicalism of his sweetly revolutionary spirit, and Diarmuid O'Murchu, whose *Quantum Theology* and *Catching Up With Jesus* are two of the most exciting books I've ever read, and J. K. Rowling, whose power to entrance readers with her tales of wizards and witches, set against the real backdrop of the Christ narrative, could surely be put to remarkable use in rethinking the gospel for our time.[8]

It doesn't really matter that they aren't all Christians, because a lot of the Christians who designed the church in earlier centuries weren't very Christian either.

Take notice, Bill Gates, Warren Buffett, Ted Turner, and the Lilly Foundation, and dream of what you could do with a few million dollars and an idea like this!

---

8. In *The Life, Death, and Resurrection of Harry Potter*, I have attempted to demonstrate how closely Rowling's books follow the patterns of the Christian story, even though she managed to avoid detection until almost the end of her series.

If I were building a string of new churches for our time, I would take a tip from Ernest Gordon's *Through the Valley of the Kwai*, a Scottish chaplain's recollection of how Allied soldiers fared in a Japanese prison camp during World War II. When the guards gave them permission to erect a chapel, they set it in the middle of their camp and chose to build it "without walls," with only some posts at the edges supporting a thatched roof, to symbolize the church's openness to everything, even its enemies. Once, Gordon said he overheard one of the workers, who was helping a companion carry a beam through the construction site, chiding his friend, "Take off yer cap, Mac, ye're in th' house o' God!"

I would want churches with as much glass as possible, and would wish them placed not in suburban paradises with manicured lawns and graceful plantings but in the midst of life's harshest circumstances, in tough neighborhoods, next to factories, munition plants, hospitals, tenement houses, rehabilitation centers, abortion clinics, strip clubs, crack joints, jails, gambling palaces, gang hangouts, centers of prostitution, police headquarters, and hospices of every kind. Our faith ought not to be bubble-wrapped, protected from jostling and insulated from where people live and breathe and suffer and make errors of judgment and commit criminal offenses, but should be hammered out day-by-day and week-by-week on the anvil of real life, forged in constant contact with the harsh realities of daily existence.

These churches wouldn't have only images of Jesus in them, but representations of Buddha and Vishnu and Manitou and Sophia and Muhammad and all the other symbols of extraordinary wisdom and transcendence that have marked the human journey toward higher spiritual consciousness. They should be multinational, multiracial, multicultural, and multi- everything else, reflecting our amazing openness and flexibility as we enter the greatest age of discovery and transformation our world has ever known.

Theologically, I would ask only one thing, that one phrase be written in fire on everything: RELATIONAL MATRIX. The phrase is Diarmuid O'Murchu's, and he has his Jesus, the one he imagines, say: "I belong to a web of relationships, the synergy that energizes every aspect of being and becoming. My core identity— and indeed, yours too—is born out of this ancient all-pervasive relationality."[9]

It is another way of saying "the kingdom of God."

If Jesus were alive and here today, he would be enthusiastic about all of this. He would give a Howard Dean scream, thrusting his fist into the air and shouting, "YES!," because this is the kind of imagination he had. He was no imitative, dim-witted, low-wattage Messiah trying to clone a new religion out of the old one, but a first-class, world-class, incisive-minded artist and activist out to remake the whole human consciousness when it came to being religious and honoring God.

But this raises immense questions, doesn't it? Do we have what it takes to follow him? Are we willing to become the risk-takers he was? Do we trust God enough to saw off the limb between us and the thick trunk of our former traditions? Are we actually capable of religious ecstasy? Can we really trust our imaginations? Does it matter?

Perhaps, in the final analysis, we should recall the words of Saint Joan, in Shaw's play, when Captain Robert de Baudricourt cautions her that the voices of God she hears are only in her imagination.

"Of course," she says, "that is how the messages of God come to us."[10]

9. O'Murchu, *Catching Up with Jesus*, 69.

10. Shaw, *Saint Joan*, 59.

"May it be so . . ."

Harvey Cox, who has always been one of my favorite theologians, says in *The Future of Faith* that "The wind of the Spirit is blowing. One indication is the upheaval that is shaking and renewing Christianity. Faith, rather than beliefs, is once again becoming its defining quality, and this reclaims what faith meant during its earliest years."[11]

Cox and I were at divinity school together. I used to see him at lunch time in the refectory—a big old room with tables and chairs where we could eat our lunches brought from home. He was always alone, seated at a table with his back to the window so he could read more easily. No one who saw him there realized what deep, creative thoughts were forming in his mind—some of which would later find expression in *The Secular City*, one of the most trenchant and popular books of its time. Eventually he would become a professor at Harvard and command the rapt attention of hundreds of bright undergraduates as well as graduate students. And he would continue to explore the rich ferment along the margins of Christianity as most of the churches practiced it.

In *Turning East* he examined the influence of Eastern religions on America's young people. In *A Feast of Fools* he described the uses of fantasy and imagination in life and religion. In *Many Mansions* he dealt with Christianity's relation to other faiths. In *Fire from Heaven* he talked about Pentecostalism, which was encircling the globe and changing the shape of Christianity in many quarters.

Because his books were easy to read and almost always seemed more engaged with what was happening in real life than with abstruse theological principles, many readers probably failed to see the overall significance of his work. They thought of him as dilettantish, light-weight, merely playful. Playful he might have

11. Cox, *The Future of Faith*, 223–24.

been, but he certainly wasn't light-weight. Now, in retrospect, we can see that he was behaving like the wise commentator in a play, say, the Stage Manager in Thornton Wilder's *Our Town*. He wasn't quite in the play, as other characters were, yet he was always there, making sense of the play, telling us what to watch for and how to think about what we'd seen and heard.

What Cox is saying in *The Future of Faith* is that everything, in the end, comes down to Spirit. The Holy Spirit, of course. The so-called "third person of the Trinity." In a way, this is what all his theology has been about—the waxing and waning of the Spirit, the playfulness of the Spirit, the presence of the Spirit in many religions, not only in Christianity. And now he tells us that it is the Spirit that really counts today, when traditional religions appear to be faltering and there is something in the air promising a more transcendent ecumenism than we have yet experienced.

We have unfortunately neglected the Holy Spirit in most of our churches, especially those that met in buildings on Main Street, USA, and had the best seats at local interfaith meetings and places of honor among the so-called "mainline" churches. We have talked about it in theology classes and referred to it in most of our creeds, but have not actually taken it seriously. Yet it was accorded a central role in the earliest history of Christianity, the Book of Acts, in which it was credited with amazing things, such as the incredible translinguistic experience of Pentecost (Acts 2:1–47), when thousands of believers from around the world of that time perfectly understood one another, even though they spoke different languages, and the remarkable dream-vision of Simon Peter on the housetop (Acts 10:1–33), when he was commanded to kill and eat animals, reptiles, and birds strictly forbidden by the Hebrew law, and understood that anything God pronounced clean was no longer out of bounds for him, not even the Gentiles to whom the Spirit then led him as a missionary.

Why have we been afraid of the Spirit and tended to disregard it in the practical dimensions of our churchmanship? Perhaps for the very reason that we have to be in charge, that it does not submit to our pedestrian control as other parts of our doctrines do. Even Martin Luther, who was surely as much a tool of the Spirit as any man who ever lived, dismissed a rival theologian by saying that he had swallowed the Holy Spirit, "feathers and all." If anything has been at the root of Pentecostalism's phenomenal spread around the globe since its birth at the Azusa Street meetings in 1903, it is its unfettered sense of the Spirit's presence and the willingness of otherwise normal, ordinary-appearing adherents to suspend their mental reservations and go with the flow, even to the point of self-humiliation. Yet most of us are prone to remain in our strait-jackets, unwilling to become "fools for Christ," to use St. Paul's words for such abandon (1 Cor 4:10).

If it was the Spirit of God moving in strange, uncanny ways in the early church that accounted for the survival and eventual triumph of Christianity in the world of that time, will it not also be the Spirit of God that seizes and uses us in the formation of new and higher forms of the inner life in our own time? Our problem, as Charles Gourgey cautions us in his deeply wise and graceful book *Judeochristianity*, is that we are always "seeking permanence in what is transitory and fleeting,"[12] while real faith, on the other hand, is eternal. We are always settling for less than that, and mistakenly allow mere *permanence* to become a substitute for what is *eternal*. This is what all our earthly religions are: initial experiences that have become permanentized and now stand in the way of our arriving at the eternal.

Gourgey, who lives in New York City, whose wife is blind, and who is nearly blind himself, gives a beautiful illustration of the kind of trust we must have in the Spirit of God if we are to grow beyond the limits of our present religious experience. "Sometimes

12. Gourgey, *Judeochristianity*, 328.

when I am with Karen," he says, "I hold her arm and let [her] dog guide both of us. The difference in sensation is immediate: a cane gives me a sense of control; the dog forces me to give up control. Cane travel is slow and deliberate; with a dog, movement is swift, and a little frightening if one is not used to it. A dog does not lead you in a straight line; it bobs and weaves, avoiding obstacles and people who might be in the way. And yet when it reaches the block's end and stops at the curb you can almost see it. A guide dog user knows what it is like to trust a force one cannot see, a movement that follows a circuitous and sometimes tortured path but that still reaches the destination."[13]

"You of little faith," Jesus was always saying to his disciples (Matt 6:30; 8:20; 14:31; 26:8; Luke 12:28). "Why are you afraid?" he asked them when he had calmed the sea. "Have you still no faith" (Mark 4:40)?

Trust, acceptance, reliance. Isn't this what it's all about—what it has *always* been about? Isn't it the *only* way to the transcendent kingdom—the complete and utter reign of God—we seek?

No, of course we haven't outgrown church. Most of us, anyway. Not the kind of church that is truly open and prepared to surrender to the Spirit of God. Not the kind the emerging-church folks are interested in.

But there is still a lot of growing to do, and that demands our renewed faith and allegiance to the way before us. We must not permanentize what we have experienced, like that fellow in the sensitivity group with Clyde Reid, but be willing to dig a grave and lay that experience to rest in order to follow the Spirit in new pathways ever before us. Only in that willingness shall we justify the church and all it has taught us. Only by dying shall we find life.

13. Ibid., 366.

8

A Belated Afterthought

The first edition of *Outgrowing Church* had been off the press only a few months when I realized that I might have been too hard on the organized church, because I suddenly found myself having an experience with a small congregation that forced me to rethink the whole subject of the book.

My wife of sixty-one years had been diagnosed with stage-four colon cancer and underwent surgery, followed by a prolonged experience of chemotherapy. Her surgery occurred in the afternoon. Late that evening, while the nurses were tending to her needs, I wandered like a lost soul through the nearly empty hospital halls and found myself entering a visitors' lounge where there was only one other person present, a large man with a friendly mien and a resonant voice.

After conversing for a few minutes with the stranger, I asked him, "Are you a minister?"

"How'd you guess?" was his reply.

He was there, I learned, to visit a member of his flock who had undergone surgery earlier in the day, and he, like I, was waiting for the nurses to complete their evening rounds in the member's room. I learned also that his church, a small United Methodist congregation, was located in the town where my wife and I lived, though he and I were meeting in a hospital in another locality. I had, in fact, never seen his church, as it was situated a few blocks off the major arteries of our town, and I was not aware of its existence.

In our discussion, I learned that this man had spent most of his working years as an Army chaplain and had accepted the pastorate of the small church after retiring from his military career.

I was so delighted with the man's voice and bearing and the description of his congregation that I decided on the spot that my wife and I should visit his church as soon as possible. The things he told me about the church sounded almost too good to be true.

But, alas, my wife never again felt comfortable about attending church, as she began chemotherapy treatments immediately after her surgery and never knew when she would be attacked by a sudden need to rush to the bathroom. And, as her sole caregiver, I never wanted to be away from our home more than the few minutes required to run to the grocery or the drugstore, so I did not visit the church alone.[1]

My wife took her final breaths late on a Saturday night in March 2014. The kind ladies from our local hospice were there to telephone the undertakers and help me tidy up things as we waited. It was 2 a.m. when everyone had left and I finally got to bed, so I did not try to get up for church the next morning. I did, however, decide that I would attend the following Sunday.

I cannot adequately describe the warmth and care of the reception I received from that small but welcoming congregation. People were not pushy. No one attempted to woo me into their membership. They all simply surrounded me in a gentle, concerned manner and assured me of their concern for my loss and my welfare.

Who were these kind and loving people?

Many were retirees who had held important positions. One of the sweetest-mannered men I met was a retired Army general whose wife and I struck up an immediate friendship because we

---

1. I have described our situation in my book *The Caregiver's Bible*.

were both writers. Another man was a retired football coach. A lovely woman I met was a former CIA agent whose deceased husband had also been employed by the agency.

I had not been attending the church more than a couple of weeks before I was invited to dinner at the home of a man who had been for twenty-five years the chief legal counsel for GEICO International. Returning to his home a few days later, I was shown his libraries—not one, not two, not three, but *four* of them in the beautiful, rambling country house where he and his wife lived.

I learned that he was an avid collector of books on many subjects. In his main library, there was a table where twelve or fifteen books lay spread out so that each was visible. He told me that he read for fifteen minutes or more each day in every book on the table. When he had read all of those books, he said, they would be replaced by others. And they were not all books of fiction—more often than not, they were books on language and science and other difficult subjects he was trying to master.

These folks were all drawn to this particular little Methodist church not because they had always been Methodists but because they had learned what an honest, loving collection of people it was and how caring they were of one another's personalities and opinions. And I am sure the unusual vitality and bonhomie of the pastor also had something to do with their being there.

The church offered two worship services each Sunday, one at 8:30 a.m. and the other at 10:45. Between services, everybody seemed to congregate in the large fellowship hall, which accommodated numerous small-group discussions and much hugging and kissing as people from the earlier service were leaving and those for the later service were arriving.

The congregation was mainly white, but there were also some blacks and Hispanics, and even one Asian woman and her little girl. One Hispanic man had applied for U.S. citizenship, and he and his American wife became immediate favorites of mine.

Each Sunday, a child between the ages of ten and fifteen served as acolyte for the services. My two favorite children performing this duty were a precocious white girl named McKenna, who soon gave me an enthusiastic hug each time she saw me, and a tall black boy named Rasheed, who with his beautifully molded hairstyle and erect posture made me think he was one of the handsomest young men I had ever seen.

Without exception, the people of the congregation were warm, friendly, open, and demonstrably loving.

Two features of the liturgy impressed me from the beginning, and continue to do so now, several years later.

One is a time when the pastor calls for the naming of joys and concerns of the congregation so that they can be noted in the communal prayer following their announcements. People ask for prayers for friends, family members, and others who are undergoing particular stress, hospital stays, or conspicuous losses in their lives. And invariably there are mentions of concerns about things that lie far from the personal affairs of the congregation—disasters at home and abroad that have been in the news, prominent people who are undergoing unusual stress or demands on their lives, upcoming legislation in Congress, and particular concerns about not only our church but other churches or church bodies worldwide.

I myself have often mentioned illnesses of friends near and far or crises faced by acquaintances as far away as California and New York and even overseas.

The other thing about our liturgical experience is the weekly communion meal, which, because the congregation is not overly large, involves people's leaving their pews and coming forward to receive a sizable piece of bread pulled from a loaf by one server and then dipping it into a cup of grape juice held by another server. I cannot describe with enough enthusiasm what this moving around by the congregation is like, with people touching or hugging one another as they pass either in the aisles or in the pews themselves. It is a mass love affair, and I always return to my seat with a sense of delight at having greeted and been greeted by so many warm and thoughtful congregants.

The communion itself is meaningful, and would have been so even without our moving about the sanctuary. But to be embraced and caressed by so many dear folks in the act of moving about is best described as heavenly.

I often confess that I have never known such a loving, intimate congregation as exists in this little church. Once, I counted all the churches to which I have belonged in my lifetime, from the one where I first became a Christian at the age of eleven to the ones I joined in various places where I was receiving my education and to the ones I later pastored, and was astounded to realize that I have been a member of no fewer than twenty churches. But never, in all of these churches—some small and some large, some mere country churches and others large, sophisticated city churches—have I found the incredible love and friendship that I have enjoyed in this one small, architecturally insignificant church hidden away on the edge of the town where I now live.

But our little church isn't just a meet-and-greet club; it is also very service-oriented. Our young people have a motel ministry to the residents of small, inexpensive motels where mainly poor people reside because rooms there are cheaper than in other housing in the community. There is a prison ministry led by the women, who enter jails to speak words of kindness and hope, and there is a computer ministry, headed by a knowledgeable techie who refurbishes discarded machines and then forwards them to poor children in Haiti and other deprived destinations. There is a prayer ministry and a hospital ministry. Teams from our church take over the restoration of decaying homes where impoverished owners live. Our people are engaged in anything judged to be helpful to the poor or rejected persons of our society. Almost every week, I discover some new or little-known projection of our congregation into the areas of greatest need in the larger community.

And our people are great about celebrating! On the first Sunday of each month, before the service begins, people's birthdays are acknowledged and we sing "Happy Birthday" to them. The women serve a tasty breakfast one morning a month, and the men regularly offer spaghetti dinners and fish dinners. There is always cheering when a member returns from a stay in the hospital or an absence for any other reason. Every Sunday, there is a festivity of kissing and hugging in the hallways and fellowship room and the sanctuary itself. Few people slip in or out without being noticed, and a sense of joy and companionship presides over everything.

Even if our services themselves weren't worshipful and restorative, which they are, I would eagerly anticipate every Sunday's gathering for the opportunity it affords to reaffirm our humanity and embrace a great variety of friends.

If I had had the experience of belonging to this wonderful little church before I wrote *Outgrowing Church*, I probably wouldn't have written the book. "Outgrowing church?" I would have thought. "I will never outgrow what I'm receiving from this delightful little congregation."

Now I am forced to rethink the premise of the book—that real, vital Christianity has largely been lost from the context of present-day churches so that most congregations, Sunday by Sunday, merely go through the motions of worship and hearing the gospel without actually experiencing anything like a restoration of the real excitement and vitality of genuine religion.

My judgment, after considerable thought, is that my premise was and is basically correct, and the book can stand on its own as a description of what most Christian religion is like today.

I had lived in this community for years before discovering the particular fellowship to which I now belong. Mine had been the repeated experience of most of the incoming population I have known, that the major churches in the town are moribund institutions that fill a certain need for many of the town's citizens who grew up here and need public organizations where they can see the folks they have always known and keep up with the latest gossip about those people. So they gather from week to week, sing the same old hymns every Sunday, and weakly fulfill their sense of belonging to an institution that owes its existence to there having once been a Savior who died on a cross and was raised to new life on the third day. If they have never known anything else, this experience, if not fulfilling, is at least a token acknowledgment of the faith of our fathers and mothers.

Most of these church members, I believe, would testify that they have had a salvation experience and will go to heaven when they die. They can probably cite the year in which they had this experience, and date their involvement with the church from that particular time in their lives.

I do not wish to be critical of these folks and their testimony. But, from my perspective as a relatively new member of the community and as a citizen of the changing world around us, I cannot give them very high marks for the lasting passion of their experiences or the continuing effectiveness of a religion that was, in its earlier years, not only life-changing but world-altering. They worship at old altars bearing the charcoaled remains of sacrifices made long, long ago and now, in many cases, covered by the cobwebs of stale, oratorical sermons and the detritus of old and outworn theologies.

How many churches did I say I had belonged to in the course of my life? Twenty? And not one of them had the freshness, passion, and vitality of the one I now attend.

I rest my case.

Maybe not all churches today bear the guilt and stigma of which I have written in this book, but most of them do. Perhaps the fact that I have at last found one church that doesn't fall under the general judgment I have brought upon churches in general hails the possibility that there are others like it.

If so, wonderful!

I can only hope this means that the witness of one church, or of a few like the one I have found, can somehow become viral and infect all the others in Christendom. It would be wonderful indeed if all the spores of our faith in its original strength and vitality would be somehow stirred up again by a mighty wind from God and bring about a revival such as the world has seldom witnessed!

But what I have said in this book still stands. On the whole, there is a lot of fakery in Christianity today—people posing as Christians and acting out the charade as if they have total confidence in God and their salvation. I don't think they are aware that they're posing. They simply do it without reflecting on it. It isn't new, of course. There have always been impostors in the flock, followers of St. Judas.

These are critical times. Many things are changing in our world—with incredible swiftness!—and they will all affect who we are and how we think as Christians. The important thing is that we think—that we not simply lie back and let everything drift along on its own, producing a church that is so identical with our culture that we cannot distinguish between church and culture, for, when that happens, we have definitely and incontrovertibly outgrown the church. Not the *real* church, of course, but the church as it exists in most of the towns and cities of our country.

Perhaps we cannot do better, at this juncture, than to pray another prayer William Cleary gave us in his *Prayers to an Evolutionary God*:

Often our prayer to you, Eternal Spirit, begins with the past,
>with memories of people
>whose love has supported us in life,
>sheltering us through every storm of circumstance,
>with gratitude for so many events
>that have warmed our hearts and enriched our days.

Yet ahead there is an unfolding future,
>which is just as remarkable as the past,
>>more so, in fact.

As you have been the empowering spirit of evolution
>for the fifteen billion years of our knowable cosmos,
>so you will energize the future
>with a wealth of events beyond our imagination.

Our prayers, then, shall turn more often into hope,
>emboldened by what we know of the past.

Guide us on this continuing journey, Holy Creating Love,
>where almost nothing is impossible.
>May it be so.[2]

---

2. Cleary, *Prayers to an Evolutionary God*, 128.

Bibliography

Armstrong, Karen. *The Battle for God*. New York: Knopf, 2000.

———. *The Case for God*. New York: Anchor, 2010.

Barna, George. *Revolution*. Carol Stream, IL: Tyndale, 2005.

Bawer, Bruce. *Stealing Jesus*. New York: Crown, 1997.

Bettenson, Henry, editor. *The Early Christian Fathers*. Oxford: Oxford University Press, 1956.

Butler Bass, Diane. *Christianity for the Rest of Us*. San Francisco: HarperSanFrancisco, 2006.

———. *A People's History of Christianity: The Other Side of the Story*. New York: HarperOne, 2009.

Butman, Harry R. *Why Do Church People Fight?* Oak Creek, WI: Congregational, 2005.

Carse, James. *Breakfast at the Victory: The Mysticism of Ordinary Experience*. San Francisco: HarperSanFrancisco, 1994.

Clark, Theodore. *Saved by His Life*. New York: Doubleday, 1959.

Claypool, John R. *Tracks of a Fellow Struggler: Living and Growing through Grief*. Waco, TX: Word, 1982.

Cleary, William. *Prayers to an Evolutionary God*. Woodstock, VT: Skylight Paths, 2002.

———. "Prayer 61: An Unfolding Future—When Feeling Conflict." In *Prayers to an Evolutionary God*, 128. With an afterword by Diarmuid O'Murchu. Woodstock, VT: SkyLight Paths, 2004

Covington, Dennis. *Salvation on Sand Mountain: Snake Handling and Redemption in Southern Appalachia*. Cambridge, MA: DaCapo, 1995.

Cox, Harvey. *The Secular City: Secularization and Urbanization in Theological Perspective*. New York: Macmillan, 1965.

———. *Feast of Fools: A Theological Essay on Festivity and Fantasy*. Cambridge, MA: Harvard University Press, 1969.

———. *Turning East: The Promise and the Peril of the New Orientalism*. New York: Simon & Schuster, 1978.

———. *Many Mansions: A Christian's Encounter with Other Faiths*. Boston: Beacon, 1988.

————. *Fire from Heaven: The Rise of Pentecostal Spirituality and the Reshaping of Religion in the 21st Century*. Cambridge, MA: DaCapo, 1994.

————. *The Future of Faith*. New York: HarperOne, 2009.

Dawkins, Richard. *The God Delusion*. Boston: Houghton Mifflin, 2006.

DeVries, Peter. *The Mackerel Plaza*. New York: Little, Brown, 1977.

Dillard, Annie. *Teaching a Stone to Talk: Expeditions and Encounters*. New York: HarperCollins, 1988.

Duin, Julia. *Quitting Church: Why the Faithful Are Fleeing and What to Do About It*. Grand Rapids: Baker, 2008.

Dunn, James D. G. *Did the First Christians Worship Jesus? The New Testament Evidence*. Louisville: Westminster John Knox, 2000.

Eadie, Betty. *Embraced by the Light*. Detroit: Gold Leaf, 1992.

Ehrman, Bart. *Forged: Writing in the Name of God: Why the Bible's Authors Are Not Who We Think They Are*. New York: HarperOne, 2011.

————. *Misquoting Jesus: The Story behind Who Changed the Bible and Why*. New York: HarperSanFrancisco, 2005.

Ellerbe, Helen. *The Dark Side of Christian History*. Orlando: Morningstar & Lark, 1995.

Fiand, Barbara. *From Religion Back to Faith: A Journey of the Heart*. Spring Valley, NY: Crossroad, 2006.

Flynn, Robert. *Growing Up a Sullen Baptist and Other Lies*. Denton: University of North Texas Press, 2001.

Fox, Matthew. *The Coming of the Cosmic Christ: The Healing of Mother Earth and the Birth of a Global Renaissance*. New York: Harper & Row, 1988.

Funk, Robert, and Roy Hoover, eds. *The Five Gospels: The Search for the Authentic Words of Jesus*. New York: Scribner, 1993.

Gibson, David. *The Coming Catholic Church: How the Faithful Are Shaping a New American Catholicism*. San Francisco: HarperSanFrancisco, 2003.

Goldstein, Niles Elliot. *God at the Edge: Searching for the Divine in Uncomfortable and Unexpected Places*. New York: Bell Tower, 2000.

Gordon, Ernest. *Through the Valley of the Kwai*. New York: Harper & Row, 1962.

Gourgey, Charles. *Judeochristianity: The Meaning and Dicovery of Faith*. Cleveland, TN: Parson's Porch, 2011.

Harris, Sam. *The End of Faith: Religion, Terror, and the Future of Reason*. New York: Norton, 2005.

————. *Letter to a Christian Nation*. New York: Knopf, 2006.

Hendricks, William D. *Exit Interviews: Revealing Stories of Why People Are Leaving the Church*. Chicago: Moody, 1993.

Henry, Patrick. *The Ironic Christian's Companion: Finding the Marks of God's Grace in the World*. New York: Riverhead, 1999.

Hitchens, Christopher. *God Is not Great: How Religion Poisons Everything*. New York: Twelve/Warner, 2007.

Hoekendyjk, J. C. *The Church Inside Out*. Edited by L. A. Hoedemaker and Pieter Tijmes. Translated by Isaac C. Rottenberg. Adventures in Faith. Philadelphia: Westminster, 1966.

Idiby, Ranya, Suzanne Oliver, and Priscilla Warner. *The Faith Club: A Muslim, a Christian, a Jew—Three Women Search for Understanding*. New York: Free Press, 2006.

Jamieson, Alan. *A Churchless Faith: Faith Journeys beyond the Churches*. London: SPCK, 2002.

Jones, W. Paul. *The Province Beyond the River: The Diary of a Protestant at a Trappist Monastery*. Nashville: Upper Room, 1981.

Kazantzakis, Nikos. *Report to Greco*. New York: Simon & Schuster, 1965.

Keen, Sam. *In the Absence of God: Dwelling in the Presence of the Sacred*. New York: Harmony, 2010.

Killinger, John. *For God's Sake, Be Human*. Waco, TX: Word, 1970.

———. *Leave It to the Spirit: A Handbook of Experimental Worship*. New York: Harper & Row, 1971.

———. *To Meet—To Touch—To Know*. Nashville: United Methodist Graded Press, 1972.

———. *The Salvation Tree*. New York: Harper & Row, 1973.

———. *Experimental Preaching*. Nashville: Abingdon, 1973.

———. *All You Lonely People, All You Lovely People*. Waco, TX: Word, 1973.

———. *The Second Coming of the Church*. Nashville: Abingdon, 1974.

———. *The Eleven O'Clock News and Other Experimental Sermons*. Nashville: Abingdon, 1975.

———. *Bread for the Wilderness, Wine for the Journey*. Waco, TX: Word, 1976.

———. *A Sense of His Presence: The Devotional Commentary on Matthew*. New York: Doubleday, 1977.

———. *His Power in You: The Devotional Commentary on Mark*. New York: Doubleday, 1978.

———. *The Gospel of Contagious Joy: A Devotional Guide to Luke*. Waco, TX: Word, 1980.

———. *The Gospel of Eternal Life: A Devotional Guide to John*. Waco, TX: Word, 1981.

———. *Prayer: The Act of Being With God*. Waco, TX: Word, 1981.

———. *Beginning Prayer*. Nashville: Upper Room, 1981; reissued 2013.

———. *A Devotional Guide to the Gospels*. Waco, TX: Word, 1984.

———. *Day by Day with Jesus: 365 Meditations on the Gospels*. Waco, TX: Word, 1984.

———. *Preaching to a Church in Crisis*. Lima, OH: CSS Publishing Company, 1995.

———. *Lost in Wonder, Love, and Praise: Prayers for Christian Worship*. Nashville: Abingdon, 2001.

———. *Enter Every Trembling Heart*. Nashville: Abingdon, 2002.

————. *Ten Things I Learned Wrong from a Conservative Church*. Spring Valley, NY: Crossroad, 2002.

————. *Winter Soulstice: Celebrating the Spirituality of the Wisdom Years*. Spring Valley, NY: Crossroad, 2005.

————. *God's People at Prayer: A Year of Prayers and Responses for Worship*. Nashville: Abingdon, 2006.

————. *The Changing Shape of Our Salvation*. Spring Valley, NY: Crossroad, 2007.

————. *The Life, Death, and Resurrection of Harry Potter*. Macon, GA: Mercer University Press, 2009.

————. *Hidden Mark: Exploring Christianity's Heretical Gospel*. Macon, GA: Mercer University Press, 2010.

————. *The Caregiver's Bible*. Warrenton, VA: Asclepion/Intermundia, 2014.

Lesser, Elizabeth. *The New American Spirituality: A Seeker's Guide*. New York: Random House, 1999.

Lyons, Gabe. *The Next Christians: Seven Ways You Can Live the Gospel and Restore the World*. New York: Doubleday, 2000.

McLaren, Brian. *A New Kind of Christian: A Tale of Two Friends on a Spiritual Journey*. San Francisco: Jossey-Bass, 2001.

————. *A New Kind of Christianity: Ten Questions That Are Transforming the Faith*. New York: HarperOne, 2010.

Melville, Herman. *Moby-Dick*. Evanston, IL: Northwestern University Press, 1988.

Menninger, Karl. *Man against Himself*. New York: Harcourt, Brace & World, 1938.

Merton, Thomas. *Seven Storey Mountain: An Autobiography of Faith*. New York: Harcourt, Brace, 1948.

Meyers, Robin R. *Saving Jesus from the Church: How to Stop Worshipping Christ and Start Following Jesus*. New York: HarperOne, 2009.

O'Murchu, Diarmuid. *Catching Up with Jesus*. Spring Valley, NY: Crossroad, 2005.

————. *Quantum Theology*. Spring Valley, NY: Crossroad, 2000.

O'Reilley, Mary Rose. *The Barn at the End of the World*. Minneapolis: Milkweed, 2000.

Pelikan, Jaroslav. *Jesus through the Centuries*. New Haven, CT: Yale University Press, 1985.

Polkinghorne, John. *Quarks, Chaos, and Christianity*. Spring Valley, NY: Crossroad, 2005.

Rawlings, Maurice. *Beyond Death's Door*. Nashville: Nelson, 1978.

Raymo, Chet. *Honey from Stone*. New York: Hungry Mind, 1987.

————. *When God Is Gone Everything Is Holy*. Notre Dame, IN: Sorin, 2008.

Redfield, James, Michael Murphy, and Sylvia Timbers. *God and the Evolving Universe*. New York: Tarcher-Putnam, 2002.

Reid, Clyde. *Celebrate the Temporary*. New York: HarperCollins, 1974.

Robinson, John A. T. *Honest to God*. Louisville: Westminster, 1962.

Sanders, Brian. *Life after Church: God's Call to Disillusioned Christians*. Downers Grove, IL: InterVarsity, 2007.

Shaw, George Bernard. *Saint Joan*. London: Constable, 1924.

Smith, Huston. *The Soul of Christianity*. San Francisco: HarperSanFrancisco, 2005.

Spencer, Michael. *Mere Churchianity*. Colorado Springs: WaterBrook Multnomah, 2001.

Spong, John Shelby. *A New Christianity for a New World*. San Francisco: HarperSanFrancsico, 2001.

———. *Why Christianity Must Change or Die*. New York: HarperCollins, 1998.

Taylor, Barbara Brown. *Leaving Church: A Memoir of Faith*. San Francisco: HarperSanFrancisco, 2006.

Tickle, Phyllis. *The Great Emergence: How Christianity Is Changing and Why*. Grand Rapids: Baker, 2008.

Wilkinson, Bruce. *The Prayer of Jabez: Breaking Through to the Blessed Life*. Sisters, OR: Multnomah, 2000.

Wuthnow, Robert. *Christianity in the 21st Century*. Oxford: Oxford University Press, 1993.

Made in the USA
Las Vegas, NV
17 July 2021